8th Workshop on Cognitive Modeling and Computational Linguistics (CMCL 2018)

Salt Lake City, Utah, USA
7 January 2018

ISBN: 978-1-5108-5550-2

Printed from e-media with permission by:

Curran Associates, Inc.
57 Morehouse Lane
Red Hook, NY 12571

Some format issues inherent in the e-media version may also appear in this print version.

Copyright© (2018) by the Association for Computational Linguistics
All rights reserved.

Printed by Curran Associates, Inc. (2018)

For permission requests, please contact the Association for Computational Linguistics
at the address below.

Association for Computational Linguistics
209 N. Eighth Street
Stroudsburg, Pennsylvania 18360

Phone: 1-570-476-8006
Fax: 1-570-476-0860

acl@aclweb.org

Additional copies of this publication are available from:

Curran Associates, Inc.
57 Morehouse Lane
Red Hook, NY 12571 USA
Phone: 845-758-0400
Fax: 845-758-2633
Email: curran@proceedings.com
Web: www.proceedings.com

Proceedings of the 8th Workshop on Cognitive Modeling and Computational Linguistics

(CMCL 2018)

January 7, 2018

Thanks to our generous sponsor:

The Department of Cognitive Science at Johns Hopkins University

Introduction

The eighth workshop in Cognitive Modelling and Computational Linguistics (CMCL 2018) was held in Salt Lake City, Utah. This time we decided to do things differently and co-locate our workshop with the first meeting of the Society for Computation in Linguistics (SCiL), which itself was held alongside the annual January meeting of the Linguistics Society of America. We did this instead of the usual workshop arrangement with an Association of Computational Linguistics (ACL) affiliated conference in order to emphasize the interdisciplinary nature of the CMCL "mission" and attract papers and attendees who do not normally attend ACL-related venues. We intend to return to ACL conferences and possibly alternate between ACL and linguistics-focused venues in the future.

We are very pleased to report that our strategy was successful. This year's proceedings cover a wide gamut of computational models and experimental techniques for linguistic and psycholinguistic phenomena, from fMRI work to language modeling for reading times. As before, we provided a Best Student Paper Award and four travel grants to student authors. Thanks to the generous support of the Department of Cognitive Science at Johns Hopkins University for enabling us to continue that tradition this year.

We received fifteen paper submissions in total, of which six were chosen for oral presentation and two for posters. One paper was chosen as an extended abstract and presented as a poster and does not appear in these proceedings. We would like to give special note to the extremely high quality of submissions relative to the limited time in our schedule; making final acceptance decisions was truly a very difficult process of choosing among excellent and interesting work.

Finally, once again, we would like to thank the authors, reviewers, and attendees for making this workshop a successful endeavour.

Cassandra Jacobs
Tal Linzen
Asad Sayeed
Marten van Schijndel

Organizers

Cassandra Jacobs, University of California at Davis; Stitch Fix
Tal Linzen, Johns Hopkins University
Asad Sayeed, University of Gothenburg
Marten van Schijndel, Johns Hopkins University

Program Committee:

Omri Abend, Hebrew University of Jerusalem
Afra Alishahi, Tilburg University
Fatemeh Torabi Asr, Indiana University
Klinton Bicknell, Northwestern University
Christos Christodoulopoulos, Amazon
Alexander Clark, King's College
Vera Demberg, University of Saarland
Brian Dillon, University of Massachusetts
Micha Elsner, The Ohio State University
Afsaneh Fazly, University of Toronto
Bob Frank, Yale University
Michael C. Frank, Stanford University
Robert Frank, Yale University
Stella Frank, Edinburgh University
Thomas Graf, Stony Brook University
John T. Hale, Cornell University
Jeffrey Heinz, University of Delaware
Tim Hunter, UCLA
Shalom Lappin, King's College
Pavel Logacev, Bogazici University
Emily Morgan, Tufts University
Timothy John O'Donnell, McGill University
Sebastian Padó, University of Stuttgart
Bozena Pajak, Duolingo
Lisa Pearl, UC Irvine
Steven Piantadosi, University of Rochester
Roi Reichart, Technion University
Brian Roark, Google
Ingeborg Roete, Max Planck Institute for Psycholinguistics
William Schuler, The Ohio State University
Cory Shain, The Ohio State University
Suzanne Stevenson, University of Toronto
Titus von der Malsburg, UCSD
Colin Wilson, Johns Hopkins University

Table of Contents

Coreference and Focus in Reading Times
Evan Jaffe, Cory Shain and William Schuler 1

Predictive power of word surprisal for reading times is a linear function of language model quality
Adam Goodkind and Klinton Bicknell 10

Dynamic encoding of structural uncertainty in gradient symbols
Pyeong Whan Cho, Matthew Goldrick, Richard L. Lewis and Paul Smolensky 19

Phonological (un)certainty weights lexical activation
Laura Gwilliams, David Poeppel, Alec Marantz and Tal Linzen 29

Predicting and Explaining Human Semantic Search in a Cognitive Model
Filip Miscevic, Aida Nematzadeh and Suzanne Stevenson 35

Modeling bilingual word associations as connected monolingual networks
Yevgen Matusevych, Amir Ardalan Kalantari Dehaghi and Suzanne Stevenson 46

Experiential, Distributional and Dependency-based Word Embeddings have Complementary Roles in Decoding Brain Activity
Samira Abnar, Rasyan Ahmed, Max Mijnheer and Willem Zuidema 57

Exactly two things to learn from modeling scope ambiguity resolution: Developmental continuity and numeral semantics
K.J. Savinelli, Greg Scontras and Lisa Pearl 67

Conference Program

Sunday, January 7, 2018

8:45–9:00   *Opening Remarks*

Oral presentations

9:00–9:30   *Coreference and Focus in Reading Times*
Evan Jaffe, Cory Shain and William Schuler

9:30–10:00   *Predictive power of word surprisal for reading times is a linear function of language model quality*
Adam Goodkind and Klinton Bicknell

10:00–10:30   *Dynamic encoding of structural uncertainty in gradient symbols*
Pyeong Whan Cho, Matthew Goldrick, Richard L. Lewis and Paul Smolensky

10:30–11:00   *Phonological (un)certainty weights lexical activation*
Laura Gwilliams, David Poeppel, Alec Marantz and Tal Linzen

11:00–11:30   *Predicting and Explaining Human Semantic Search in a Cognitive Model*
Filip Miscevic, Aida Nematzadeh and Suzanne Stevenson

11:30–12:00   *Modeling bilingual word associations as connected monolingual networks*
Yevgen Matusevych, Amir Ardalan Kalantari Dehaghi and Suzanne Stevenson

Poster presentations

12:00–12:30   *Experiential, Distributional and Dependency-based Word Embeddings have Complementary Roles in Decoding Brain Activity*
Samira Abnar, Rasyan Ahmed, Max Mijnheer and Willem Zuidema

12:00–12:30   *Exactly two things to learn from modeling scope ambiguity resolution: Developmental continuity and numeral semantics*
K.J. Savinelli, Greg Scontras and Lisa Pearl

12:00–12:30   *Uniform Information Density (UID) Effects on Syntactic Choice in Hindi and English* [extended abstract]
A. Jain, V. Singh, S. Agarwal, R. Rajkumar

Coreference and Focus in Reading Times

Evan Jaffe
Department of Linguistics
The Ohio State University
`jaffe.59@osu.edu`

Cory Shain
Department of Linguistics
The Ohio State University
`shain.3@osu.edu`

William Schuler
Department of Linguistics
The Ohio State University
`schuler.77@osu.edu`

Abstract

This paper presents evidence of a linguistic focus effect on coreference resolution in broad-coverage human sentence processing. While previous work has explored the role of prominence in coreference resolution (Almor, 1999; Foraker and McElree, 2007), these studies use constructed stimuli with specific syntactic patterns (e.g. cleft constructions) which could have idiosyncratic frequency confounds. This paper explores the generalizability of this effect on coreference resolution in a broad-coverage analysis. In particular, the current work proposes several new estimators of prominence appropriate for broad-coverage sentence processing and evaluates them as predictors of reading behavior in the Natural Stories corpus (Futrell, Gibson, Tily, Vishnevetsky, Piantadosi, and Fedorenko, in prep), a collection of "constructed-natural" narratives read by a large number of subjects. Results show a strong facilitation effect for one of these predictors on exploratory data and confirm that it generalizes to held-out data. These results provide broad-coverage support for the hypothesis that coreference resolution is easier when the target entity is focused by discourse properties, resulting in faster reading times.

1 Introduction

Coreference resolution has often been assumed to incur processing costs due to some form of memory retrieval or search through accessible antecedents, similar to the binding problem for syntactic dependency attachment (Felser, Phillips, and Wagers 2017). This search has been shown to be facilitated by linguistic focus (or prominence or salience) arising from syntactic, pragmatic, semantic, lexical, information structural and other factors. Previous work has investigated the role of linguistic focus in coreference resolution using constructed stimuli (Perfetti and Goldman, 1974; Greene et al., 1992; Almor, 1999; Foraker and McElree, 2007). However, as discussed in Shain et al. (2016), effects found using constructed stimuli often fail to generalize to broad-coverage sentence processing. It is possible that results obtained using constructed stimuli are due in part to (1) information-theoretic factors that such studies rarely control for (e.g. surprisal), (2) limited syntactic coverage, and/or (3) properties of the stimuli themselves that are atypical of naturalistic sentence processing (e.g. overrepresentation of rare constructions, odd semantics, or lack of context).

While previous work (Almor, 1999; Foraker and McElree, 2007) has operationalized prominence or linguistic focus using cleft constructions, such constructions are very rare (Roland et al., 2007) and therefore cannot be relied upon to predict online processing in the broad-coverage setting.

The current work addresses these concerns by deploying novel broad-coverage implementations of focus as predictors of reading times in a large corpus of naturalistic self-paced reading (SPR) by many subjects (Futrell, Gibson, Tily, Vishnevetsky, Piantadosi, and Fedorenko, in prep). Following Shain et al. (2016), the current work evaluates these predictors against a baseline including both n-gram and probabilistic context-free grammar (PCFG) estimates of incremental surprisal. Using this procedure, results show a significant facilitatory effect of predictors relating to linguistic focus on reading time latencies, supporting the hypothesis that focus effects for coreference observed using constructed stimuli do indeed gener-

1

Proceedings of the 8th Workshop on Cognitive Modeling and Computational Linguistics (CMCL 2018), pages 1–9,
Salt Lake City, Utah, USA, January 7, 2018. ⓒ2018 Association for Computational Linguistics

alize to broad-coverage sentence processing.

2 Related Work

The current study draws on two broad areas of investigation in the psycholinguistic literature: (1) the role of linguistic focus in coreference resolution and (2) the use of broad-coverage methods to test models of human sentence processing.

2.1 Linguistic focus and coreference resolution

Linguistic focus directs subjects' attention toward particularly salient or important discourse referents during sentence processing. Studies such as Perfetti and Goldman (1974), Greene et al. (1992), Almor (1999), Foraker and McElree (2007) and Sauermann et al. (2013) have explored the effects of linguistic focus on subjects' processing of coreference.

Greene et al. (1992) offer a model of pronoun resolution within a rich discourse representation that recognizes syntactic, semantic, and pragmatic factors for referent focus. Syntactic factors that can increase focus include clefting (e.g., *It was the **bird** that ate the fruit*), subject vs. object position (e.g., *The **bird** ate the fruit*), predicative vs. prenominal modification (e.g., *the red house is **beautiful***), and the status of nouns introduced as verbal complements vs. nominal compounds (e.g., *The **boat** is located in the boathouse*). Semantic and pragmatic factors include the causal role of a referent, where the perceived causal agent of a verb could be more focused than the verb's other arguments. Additionally, referents more closely related to the topic can increase focus for those referents. The Greene et al. model matches features of each anaphor automatically and in parallel to the features of all the entities in the discourse. If the match of one entity is sufficiently high, the entity is chosen, otherwise resolution is delayed or additional inference might occur.

Almor (1999) argues for a discourse focus effect in a self-paced reading paradigm. For example, Almor uses *it*-clefts to focus the subject: *It was the robin that ate the fruit. The bird seemed quite satisfied;* and *wh*-clefts to focus the object: *What the robin ate was the fruit. The bird seemed quite satisfied.* In a self-paced reading (SPR) experiment, subsequent mentions of focused referents are read more quickly.

Foraker and McElree (2007) use a speed-accuracy tradeoff (SAT) paradigm (Wicklegren, 1977) to explore the relationship between prominence and processing cost. Referents are made more prominent using constructed *it*-cleft stimuli, as in Almor (1999). They find improved accuracy for retrieval of prominent referents but — contrary to Almor (1999) — no effect on access speed.

Sturt and Lombardo (2005) explore the time course of coreference resolution, showing evidence that syntactic structure is available before the end of the utterance, and therefore that coreference decisions are plausibly occurring in an online and incremental way. They find that eye-tracking data for sentences like *The pilot embarrassed Mary and put himself/herself/him/her in a very awkward situation,* show distinct patterns between the reflexive and simple pronoun conditions, indicating that syntactic structure is available and influencing processing even before the end of the sentence. Findings like these motivate our use of SPR as a measure of incremental processing difficulty in coreference resolution.

While the present study relies on the aforementioned approaches in operationalizing focus, it extends earlier work by using coreference-based focus predictors in broad-coverage naturalistic reading and in so doing explores implementations of focus that are better adapted to broad-coverage analysis.

2.2 Broad-coverage investigation of human sentence processing

As discussed in Section 1, naturalistic stimuli have an advantage over task-specific constructed stimuli in terms of ecological validity. Several previous studies have investigated sentence processing using naturalistic stimuli. This work typically uses linear mixed-effects modeling (LME) to regress variables of interest as predictors of some measure of processing difficulty (e.g. reading fixation times). Demberg and Keller (2008) examine syntactic dependency length as a predictor of eye-tracking fixation durations during reading of the newspaper texts contained in the Dundee corpus (Kennedy et al., 2003). They do not replicate the locality effects found in constructed experiments (Gibson, 2000; Grodner and Gibson, 2005) except when the analysis is restricted to certain parts of speech. Frank and Bod (2011) use echo state networks to compare the fit of linear vs. hierarchical probabilistic language models to eye-tracking fixation durations, finding no significant contribution of hierarchy to model fit. Van Schijndel et al. (2013) implement a measure of memory retrieval cost built on a left-corner parsing strategy and find a significant *facilitation* effect for retrieval cost on the Dundee corpus, such that tokens predicted to require more costly retrieval operations were integrated more quickly during reading.

In all of the aforementioned studies, effects obtained using constructed stimuli do not generalize to naturalistic sentence comprehension. Exceptions exist, however. For example, Shain et al. (2016) show the predicted inhibitory effect of dependency length on reading times in the Natural Stories corpus (also used in the current experiments), and Brennan et al. (2016) and Lopopolo et al. (2017) find increased neural response in certain brain regions[1] to various types of probabilistic language models. To our knowledge, the current work is the first to extend these broad-coverage methods to the study of coreference resolution.

3 Data

The experiments described in this paper use the Natural Stories corpus (Futrell, Gibson, Tily, Vishnevetsky, Piantadosi, and Fedorenko, in prep), which consists of 10 stories with reading times from 181 subjects using a self-paced reading (SPR) paradigm. These stories occupy an intermediary position between isolated constructed examples on the one hand and naturally-occurring text on the other. They are written in order to sound fluent while containing an unusually high proportion of low-frequency words and syntactic constructions which are intended to test the effects of different kinds of memory usage. The corpus contains 485 sentences with 768,023 total events, where an event is one subject reading one word. Reading times exceeding two standard deviations from the subject mean, shorter than 100ms, or longer than 3000ms are excluded as outliers.

For this work, the data is divided into 1/3 development or exploratory and 2/3 test or confirmatory partitions. All main effects are evaluated first on exploratory data, and the optimal main effect (in terms of improvement to model fit over the baseline) is then selected for evaluation on confirmatory data. This data split allows for the optimiza-

tion of model predictors and parameters on the exploratory set, and eliminates the need for multiple trials correction since only one model is applied to the confirmatory partition.

3.1 Coreference Annotation

The current work marks all mentions that are coreferential, in contrast to many previous studies of coreference that are restricted to pronominal coreference. This allows the model to be run on all instances of coreference as well as a pronoun-only subset of the data. Due to model convergence issues for the pronoun-only subset, however, reported results are for the larger dataset of all anaphoric expressions, including pronouns and full referring forms.

All words referring to the same entity or subsets of previously mentioned sets of entities are annotated with the sentence and word index of the most recent previous mention of that entity. See Fig. 1 for example annotations. Annotation guidelines largely follow those from the OntoNotes 5.0 corpus (Weischedel et al., 2013) for identity coreference, except that (1) possessive pronouns are included in annotations, and (2) referents are associated with referring words rather than constituent spans. For example, where the OntoNotes guidelines link *a good suggestion* to *it* in the sentence, *She had a good suggestion and it was unanimously accepted*, the current annotation links the referring word, *suggestion* to the anaphor *it*.[2]

The current annotation also adds possessive determiners like *his, her, its*, which are not included in the OntoNotes identity coreference guidelines. For this study, it is assumed that such determiners require some kind of coreference resolution similar to that required for identity coreference. It is possible that a range of coreference types from strict identity coreference to more weakly related bridging anaphora, for example, would involve different processing strategies, but annotations of these distinctions is substantially more complex and left for future work.

---

[1]As measured by fMRI blood oxygen level dependent contrast imaging (BOLD)

[2]Because the reading time data is measured by word, mention spans that include multiple words would be difficult to use. That is, there is no clear procedure for assigning credit for observed latencies to the various predictors that are involved in the span. Essentially, because both the predictors and observed reading times are defined in terms of words, so must be the coreference annotation. Therefore, for multi-word mentions, the referring word is chosen.

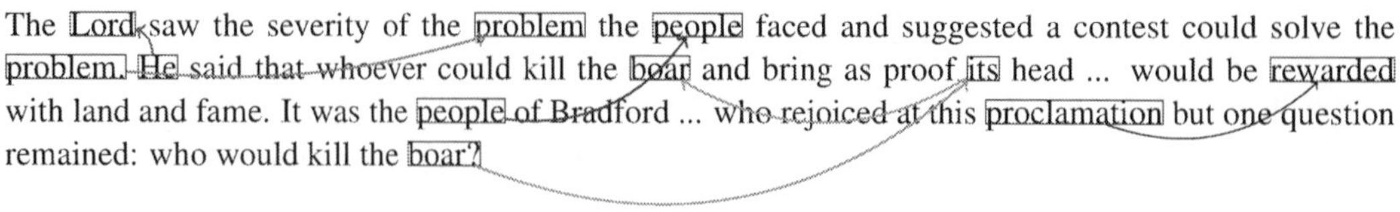

The $\boxed{\text{Lord}_i}$ saw the severity of the $\boxed{\text{problem}}$ the $\boxed{\text{people}}$ faced and suggested a contest could solve the $\boxed{\text{problem}}$. $\boxed{\text{He}}$ said that whoever could kill the $\boxed{\text{boar}}$ and bring as proof $\boxed{\text{its}}$ head ... would be $\boxed{\text{rewarded}}$ with land and fame. It was the $\boxed{\text{people of Bradford}}$ ... who rejoiced at this $\boxed{\text{proclamation}}$ but one question remained: who would kill the $\boxed{\text{boar}}$?

Figure 1: Example coreference annotation. Words in rectangles are linked to the most recent previous mention.

	The	Lord_i	saw	the	severity	of	the	problem_j	the	people	faced	and	suggested	a	contest	could	solve	the	problem_j.
MentionCount	0	0	0	0	0	0	0	0	0	0	0	0	0	0	0	0	0	0	**1**
WordDistance	0	0	0	0	0	0	0	0	0	0	0	0	0	0	0	0	0	0	**10**
ReferentDistance	0	0	0	0	0	0	0	0	0	0	0	0	0	0	0	0	0	0	**5**

	He_i	said	that	whoever	could	kill	the	boar_k	and	bring	as	proof	its_k	head	would	be	rewarded	with	land	and	fame.
MentionCount	**1**	0	0	0	0	0	0	0	0	0	0	0	**1**	0	0	0	0	0	0	0	0
WordDistance	**18**	0	0	0	0	0	0	0	0	0	0	0	**4**	0	0	0	0	0	0	0	0
ReferentDistance	**9**	0	0	0	0	0	0	0	0	0	0	0	**2**	0	0	0	0	0	0	0	0

Table 1: Example predictor values. MentionCount is the number of previous mentions to the same referent. The two other predictors measure distance in words or referents, respectively, back to the antecedent. Words sharing a subscript value are coreferential.

3.2 Baseline Predictors

In order to isolate new effects, it is necessary to statistically control for known effects. These experiments use word length, n-gram surprisal, syntactic surprisal, and story position.

Word length is a baseline predictor measured as the number of characters in each word. Longer words are predictive of longer reading times.

Surprisal (Hale, 2001) is the log of the inverse frequency, which increases as the frequency decreases. The log transform makes surprisal a more linear measure of exponential changes in stimulus. The linearity of surprisal is desirable not only because it allows LMER fitting, but because it corresponds with the Weber-Fechner law (Fechner, 1966), which maintains that perception of stimuli increase additively as stimulus strength increases multiplicatively. Stevens' power law (Stevens, 1957) expresses a similar relationship. For word frequencies, which exhibit a Zipfian curve, the log of the probability essentially converts the frequencies to a linear perception curve, allowing easier differentiation of the relative rarity of words that occur exponentially more or less frequently.

Ngram Surprisal controls for conditional word frequency, given preceding words as context, and is a commonly used baseline effect (Monsalve et al., 2012; van Schijndel and Schuler, 2015). 5-gram probability is calculated as the linear combination of most likely n-grams up to 5 words long, including the target word. Because longer n-grams are often infrequent and thus have poor or non-existent frequency estimates, Kneser-Ney smoothing allows the full sequence to be estimated as an interpolation of shorter n-grams. Following Shain et al. (2016), this work uses 5-gram probabilities from the Gigaword 4.0 corpus (Graff and Cieri, 2003) using the KenLM toolkit (Heafield et al., 2013):

$$S(w_i) = -\log P(w_i | w_{i-n}...w_{i-1}) \quad (1)$$

To control for the effect of surprisal due to syntactic context, the current work estimates the probability of syntactic tree structure at each given word (Shain et al., 2016; van Schijndel and Schuler, 2015). Syntactic context is defined as the linear combination of all previous syntactic rule productions up to the current word.

Probabilistic Context-Free Grammar (PCFG) Surprisal follows that used by van Schijndel and Schuler (2015) and comes from an incremental parser (van Schijndel et al., 2013) using the Generalized Categorial Grammar (GCG) framework of Nguyen et al. (2012). Specifically, PCFG surprisal is defined as the sum of negative log probabilities of words given possible trees that span from the first word to the current word. This is analogous to n-gram surprisal, but uses hierarchic tree context rather than linear context:

$$S(w_i) = - log\, P(T_i = w_i | T_1...T_{i-1} = w_1...w_{i-1})$$
(2)

where T is a random variable over all trees and $T_1...T_i$ are its first i leaf nodes.

Story Position is a measure of progress through the story, where each value is computed as the current sentence index divided by the total number of sentences in the story. For example, the 50th sentence in a 100 sentence story would have a story position of 0.5 for each word in that sentence. This predictor could be interpreted as a percent completion measure that is intended to model order effects due to fatigue, practice or environmental factors, and generally control for a base rate of reading as the story progresses. There is potential for discourse predictability to also be captured with the baseline predictor, analogous to sentence position but generalized to the discourse level, where the space of possible continuations decreases as more information becomes available.

Sentence Position was originally included in the baseline, but was removed as the weakest predictor in order to overcome model convergence issues.

3.3 Broad-coverage implementations of focus

Because naturalistic stimuli in English rarely contain the kinds of constructions used to control linguistic focus in constructed stimulus experiments (Roland et al., 2007), it is necessary to implement focus in some other way. This work explores two types of implementations: frequency-based and recency-based.

The frequency-based implementation, *Mention-Count*, is calculated as the running count of mentions in a coreference chain. The first mention has count 0, the subsequent mention count 1, and so on. This measure is closely related to the notion of *thematization* used in Perfetti and Goldman (1974), who also use repetition as an index of focus. As a predictor, *MentionCount* is meant to test the hypothesis that more frequent referents are faster to access. Incidentally, *Mention-Count* is quite similar to the measures of *topicality* proposed by Givón (1983), suggesting a potential connection between the discourse notion of topicality and the attendant psychological effects that is left for future research.

The recency-based implementations follow e.g.

McElree (2001) in assuming that more recently mentioned entities are more prominent and thus more likely to be remembered better. Specifically, these experiments use two measures of the distance between the current word and the most recent mention of its referent: number of intervening words, and number of intervening discourse referents. Following Gibson (2000) discourse referents are operationalized in the latter option as nouns or verbs, here including pronouns and non-finite verbs. Experiments also evaluate log-transformed versions of each of these distance measures, modeling the possibility of non-linear decay over time in likelihood that linguistic focus for mentioned entities results in processing facilitation.

Table 1 shows example values for the Mention-Count and word- and referent-based recency predictors. Log transformed versions of the recency predictors are not shown in this figure. For the first sentence, *problem* is mentioned twice. The first mention has zero previous mentions, while the second has one. Distance in words is 10 between the two mentions, and distance in referents (nouns and verbs) is 5.

4 Statistical evaluation

Each main effect predictor is evaluated on the exploratory data via likelihood ratio test (LRT) of two fitted linear mixed effects (LME) models, one including the main effect as a fixed effect and one excluding it. Both models also contain a set of baseline fixed effects: word length, 5-gram forward surprisal, incremental PCFG surprisal, and story position. All models include all baseline fixed effects. Models also include by-subject random slopes for the main effect and every baseline effect, with the exception of syntactic surprisal, whose by-subject random slopes were removed as the weakest predictor in order to overcome lack of convergence.

Experiments evaluate each main effect over all instances of coreference, as the smaller pronoun-only subset did not converge reliably.

Delays in the time course of processing effects can be modeled by spillover (Erlich and Rayner, 1983), where the effect of an independent variable is predicted to be observed n words later. Using standard linear regression on the exploratory dataset, we found the best-fit spillover position of the baseline predictors to be zero (*in situ*) with the exception of PCFG surprisal, which is optimally

	Effect Size (ms)	
Effect	Predictor units	SD
Word Length	2.17	4.23
Syntactic Surprisal	0.36	1.65
5-gram Surprisal	2.34	3.57
Story Position	-19.2	-6.62
MentionCount***	-0.14	-2.81

Table 2: Effect sizes for main and baseline predictors on confirmatory partition of data. The main effect, spilled over MentionCount, is highly significant ($p = 7.05e - 5$). Negative effect direction indicates a speed-up in reading times. SD shows β-effect in milliseconds per unit of standard deviation. Predictor Units are the effect size in milliseconds, rescaled to the original predictors' units. Model includes observations from spilled over anaphors, totaling 59,632 observations. Word Length is measured in characters, Surprisal is measured in bits, and Story Position is the proportion of sentences completed, scaled between 0 and 1.

spilled over by 1 position. In addition to optimizing the baseline predictors, we consider both *in situ* and spillover-1 variants of each of our main effects.[3]

The reading time measures are transformed following Box and Cox (1964) to match assumptions of normality by the likelihood ratio test. These experiments use a coefficient of λ = -0.63.[4] All predictors are also centered and z-transformed prior to regression.

---

[3]The reason for choosing a single optimal spillover position for each variable rather than considering multiple spillover positions simultaneously (as in Smith and Levy, 2013, for example) is that our data are too sparse to support such highly parameterized models given that we are controlling for heterogeneity in the population via by-subject random slopes for each independent variable. Since there are 181 subjects in the dataset, each additional independent variable (including each additional modeled spillover position for a given independent variable) contributes 181 additional slopes to estimate.

[4]The effect estimates given in Table 2 are presented in milliseconds for expository purposes. However, this is in fact a back-transformation of β into milliseconds using the equation β-ms $= (\lambda \bar{y}' + \lambda\beta + 1)^{1/\lambda} - (\lambda \bar{y}' + 1)^{1/\lambda}$, where $\bar{y}'$ is the mean of the transformed reading times (1.55 in our data). Because Box and Cox (1964) introduces non-linearity, β-ms is only valid at the back-transformed mean, holding all other effects at their means.

5 Results

MentionCount in the spilled-over position is highly significant on exploratory data. Results for recency-based predictors in the exploratory data partition are extremely weak, and so they are not evaluated on confirmatory data.

Due to the separation of data into exploratory and confirmatory partitions, and subsequent testing on confirmatory data only once, no multiple trials correction is required. Our results are consistent with a general pattern of smaller effect estimates in naturalistic vs. constructed studies of human sentence processing (Demberg and Keller, 2008; Smith and Levy, 2013; van Schijndel and Schuler, 2015; Shain et al., 2016). It might be the case that relatively muted tendencies in naturalistic human sentence processing are exaggerated in artificial settings devoid of conversation context or the implicit intended use of language for communication. The MentionCount values range from 0 to 90, with $\mu = 2.4$ and $SD = 9.3$. The baseline predictors all have plausible effect estimates. The Word length effect is positive, as expected, indicating a slowdown as word length increases. The linear 5-gram and hierarchic syntactic surprisal effects are both positive, indicating that processing difficulty increases with unpredictability of the current token given its context. Story position effect is negative, showing a general decrease in reading times as the story progresses.

As a sanity check, a simpler linear only model (no random effects) was run with the baseline predictors but not MentionCount. Figure 2 presents the residuals mapped to the MentionCount predictor value, showing a slight negative trend that demonstrates that for high values of MentionCount, the baseline's predictions of reading times are too high. This negative correlation between MentionCount and reading times is evident in the full LMER result. Additionally, there is no obvious confound from excessive residuals being due to items at any given MentionCount value.

6 Discussion

These results complement previous work on coreference resolution in constructed stimuli by providing strong evidence of a broad-coverage discourse focus effect on coreference resolution. The implementation of linguistic focus that successfully improved model fit was based on frequency rather than recency of mention. This is a potentially im-

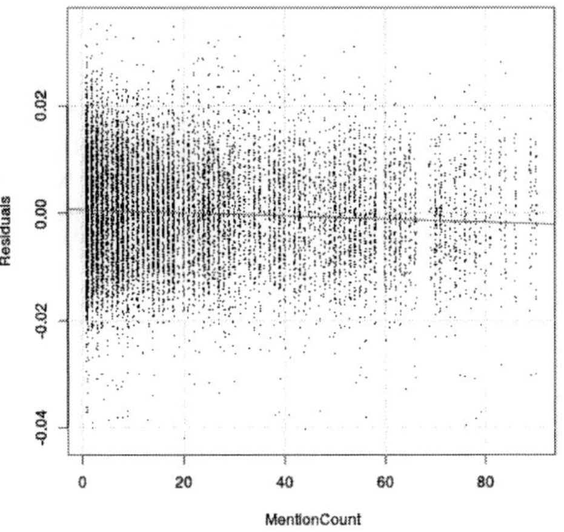

Figure 2: Scatterplot of residuals from simple linear model (no random effects) without Mention-Count plotted to spilled-over MentionCount predictor. Fit line shows slight downward trend, indicating main effect of MentionCount to reduce reading times.

portant secondary finding, since recency-based effects were found in syntactic dependency locality effects (Shain et al., 2016). The current negative result for coreference-based recency effects does coincide with related lack of recency effects for syntactic dependencies from Demberg and Keller (2008) (who also used somewhat naturalistic stimuli), and could be attributable to a number of factors. It is possible that a hybrid estimator — taking into account both recency and frequency of mention — might show stronger effects than those presented here. Additionally, since proforms are unlikely to occur at great distance to their antecedents, separating recency effects by anaphor type (full-referring vs. proform) could result in better predictors. Lastly, recency effects might be weak at short to moderate distances where coreference succeeds, but could increase in strength for constructed stimuli where the pronouns are used further from antecedents than is normal, and initial coreference fails, resulting in reanalysis. Of course, these unnatural recency effects would not be detectable or applicable when analyzing naturalistic stimuli.

It is possible that what we have interpreted as a linguistic focus effect is in fact related to surprisal. If subjects are attempting to predict discourse mentions in advance, it is possible that they are reallocating probability mass to mentions of entities as a function of the number of times they have been mentioned in the past, thereby reducing surprisal and facilitating processing of mentions consistent with this prediction. Whether the effect is indeed driven by focus or is instead driven by prediction is also left to future research.

Finally, after considering that high values of MentionCount can only exist toward the end of stories, we considered a potential confound of story position, or relative completion of the story. Story position turns out to be an extremely strong predictor that we argue should be added to future baselines for this type of data. Despite this, spilled-over MentionCount is still highly significant over this more rigorous baseline.

7 Conclusion

This work provides evidence of a linguistic focus effect based on reading time latencies from a coreference-annotated corpus of naturalistic stimuli. Experiments on naturalistic stimuli suggest that mention count is a plausible broad-coverage implementation of linguistic focus and show that more mentions of an entity are correlated with faster reading times.

Acknowledgments

Thank you to four anonymous reviewers for excellent feedback. This material is based upon work supported by the National Science Foundation Graduate Research Fellowship Program under grant no. DGE-1343012, and NSF grant no. 1551313. Any opinion, findings, and conclusions or recommendations expressed in this material are those of the author(s) and do not necessarily reflect the views of the National Science Foundation.

References

Amit Almor. 1999. Noun-phrase anaphora and focus: The informational load hypothesis. *Psychological Review* 106(4):748–765.

George E. P. Box and David R. Cox. 1964. An analysis of transformations. *Journal of the Royal Statistical Society. Series B (Methodological)* 26(2):211–252. http://www.jstor.org/stable/2984418.

Jonathan R. Brennan, Edward P. Stabler, Sarah E. Van Wagenen, Wen-Ming Luh, and John T.

Hale. 2016. Abstract linguistic structure correlates with temporal activity during naturalistic comprehension. *Brain and Language* 157:81 – 94. https://doi.org/10.1016/j.bandl.2016.04.008.

Vera Demberg and Frank Keller. 2008. Data from eye-tracking corpora as evidence for theories of syntactic processing complexity. *Cognition* 109(2):193–210.

Kate Erlich and Keith Rayner. 1983. Pronoun assignment and semantic integration during reading: Eye movements and immediacy of processing. *Journal of Verbal Learning & Verbal Behavior* 22:75–87.

Gustav Theodor Fechner. 1966. *Elements of psychophysics Elemente der Psychophysik*, volume 1. United States of America: Holt, Rinehart and Winston.

Stephani Foraker and Brian McElree. 2007. The role of prominence in pronoun resolution: Active versus passive representations. *Journal of Memory and Language* 56(3):357–383. https://doi.org/10.1016/j.jml.2006.07.004.

Stefan Frank and Rens Bod. 2011. Insensitivity of the human sentence-processing system to hierarchical structure. *Psychological Science* .

Edward Gibson. 2000. The dependency locality theory: A distance-based theory of linguistic complexity. In *Image, language, brain: Papers from the first mind articulation project symposium*. MIT Press, Cambridge, MA, pages 95–126.

Talmy Givón. 1983. Topic continuity in discourse: An introduction. In Talmy Givón, editor, *Topic Continuity in Discourse: A Quantitative Cross-Language Study*, John Benjamins, Amsterdam, pages 1–41.

David Graff and Christopher Cieri. 2003. *English Gigaword LDC2003T05*.

Steven B. Greene, Gail McKoon, and Roger Ratcliff. 1992. Pronoun resolution and discourse models. *Journal of Experimental Psychology: Learning, Memory, & Cognition* 18:266–283.

Daniel J. Grodner and Edward Gibson. 2005. Consequences of the serial nature of linguistic input. *Cognitive Science* 29:261–291.

John Hale. 2001. A probabilistic earley parser as a psycholinguistic model. In *Proceedings of the second meeting of the North American chapter of the Association for Computational Linguistics*. Pittsburgh, PA, pages 159–166.

Kenneth Heafield, Ivan Pouzyrevsky, Jonathan H. Clark, and Philipp Koehn. 2013. Scalable modified Kneser-Ney language model estimation. In *Proceedings of the 51st Annual Meeting of the Association for Computational Linguistics*. Sofia, Bulgaria, pages 690–696.

Alan Kennedy, James Pynte, and Robin Hill. 2003. The Dundee corpus. In *Proceedings of the 12th European conference on eye movement*.

Alessandro Lopopolo, Stefan L. Frank, Antal van den Bosch, and Roel M. Willems. 2017. Using stochastic language models (slm) to map lexical, syntactic, and phonological information processing in the brain. *PLOS ONE* 12(5):1–18. https://doi.org/10.1371/journal.pone.0177794.

Brian McElree. 2001. Working memory and focal attention. *Journal of Experimental Psychology, Learning Memory and Cognition* 27(3):817–835.

Irene Fernandez Monsalve, Stefan L. Frank, and Gabriella Vigliocco. 2012. Lexical surprisal as a general predictor of reading time. In *Proceedings of the 13th Conference of the European Chapter of the Association for Computational Linguistics*. Association for Computational Linguistics, Stroudsburg, PA, USA, EACL '12, pages 398–408. http://dl.acm.org/citation.cfm?id=2380816.2380866.

Luan Nguyen, Marten van Schijndel, and William Schuler. 2012. Accurate unbounded dependency recovery using generalized categorial grammars. In *Proceedings of the 24th International Conference on Computational Linguistics (COLING '12)*. Mumbai, India, pages 2125–2140.

Charles A. Perfetti and Susan R. Goldman. 1974. Thematization and sentence retrieval. *Journal of Verbal Learning and Verbal Behavior* 13(1):70 – 79. https://doi.org/http://dx.doi.org/10.1016/S0022-5371(74)80032-0.

Douglas Roland, Frederic Dick, and Jeffrey L Elman. 2007. Frequency of basic english grammatical structures: A corpus analysis. *Journal of memory and language* 57 3:348–379.

Antje Sauermann, Ruth Filik, and Kevin B. Paterson. 2013. Processing contextual and lexical cues to focus: Evidence from eye movements in reading. *Language and Cognitive Processes* 28(6):875–903. https://doi.org/10.1080/01690965.2012.668197.

Cory Shain, Marten van Schijndel, Richard Futrell, Edward Gibson, and William Schuler. 2016. Memory access during incremental sentence processing causes reading time latency. *COLING 2016, workshop on Computational Linguistics for Linguistic Complexity* .

Nathaniel J. Smith and Roger Levy. 2013. The effect of word predictability on reading time is logarithmic. *Cognition* 128:302–319.

Stanley Smith Stevens. 1957. On the psychophysical law. *Psychological Review* 64(3):153–181.

Patrick Sturt and Vincent Lombardo. 2005. Processing coordinate structures: Incrementality and connectedness. *Cognitive Science* 29:291–305.

Marten van Schijndel, Andy Exley, and William Schuler. 2013. A model of language processing as hierarchic sequential prediction. *Topics in Cognitive Science* 5(3):522–540.

Marten van Schijndel and William Schuler. 2015. Hierarchic syntax improves reading time prediction. In *Proceedings of NAACL-HLT 2015*. Association for Computational Linguistics.

R. Weischedel, M. Palmer, M. Marcus, E. Hovy, S. Pradhan, L. Ramshaw, N. Xue, A. Taylor, J. Kaufman, M. Franchini, El-Bachouti M., Belvin R., and A. Houston. 2013. Ontonotes release 5.0. `https://catalog.ldc.upenn.edu/ldc2013t19`. LDC Catalog No.: LDC2013T19.

Wayne Wicklegren. 1977. Speed-accuracy tradeoff and information processing dynamics. *Acta Psychologica* 41:67–85.

Predictive power of word surprisal for reading times is a linear function of language model quality

Adam Goodkind and **Klinton Bicknell**
Department of Linguistics
Northwestern University
Evanston, IL 60208
a.goodkind@u.northwestern.edu kbicknell@northwestern.edu

Abstract

Within human sentence processing, it is known that there are large effects of a word's probability in context on how long it takes to read it. This relationship has been quantified using information-theoretic surprisal, or the amount of new information conveyed by a word. Here, we compare surprisals derived from a collection of language models derived from n-grams, neural networks, and a combination of both. We show that the models' psychological predictive power improves as a tight linear function of language model *linguistic* quality. We also show that the size of the effect of surprisal is estimated consistently across all types of language models. These findings point toward surprising robustness of surprisal estimates and suggest that surprisal estimated by low-quality language models are not biased.

1 Introduction

Decades of work studying human sentence processing have demonstrated that a word's probability in context is strongly related to the amount of time it takes to read it. This relationship has been quantified by surprisal theory (Hale, 2001; Levy, 2008), which states that processing difficulty of a word w in context c is proportional to its information-theoretic *surprisal*, defined as $-\log p(w|c)$. As a word is more likely to occur in its context, and thus communicates less information (Shannon, 1948), it is read more quickly.

One difficulty in testing such effects of a word's probability in context is the need to construct estimates of a word's probability in context. One way of estimating such probabilities is to give human subjects a context, have them guess the next word, and estimate $p(w|c)$ as the proportion of participants who guess word w in context c. This method, called a Cloze task (Taylor, 1953), may yield reliable estimates for words that have relatively high probabilities in their context, and it has been used in a number of studies of the effects of probabilities in context on reading. However, it is an open question whether these human guess-derived proportions may be biased from objective probabilities in some way (Smith & Levy, 2011). Problematically for studying surprisal specifically, however, the Cloze task cannot in principle yield reliable estimates of word probabilities in context that are relatively low, say less than 1 in 100, as many word probabilities are, without requiring an extremely large number of participants (Levy, 2008). Additionally, it is not practical to use the Cloze task to estimate probabilities for large datasets on which surprisal is often studied, for which there can easily be tens of thousands of contexts that would require estimation.

The alternative is to estimate the probabilities of words in context using computational *language models*, which are trained on large language corpora to estimate the probabilities of words in context. Many studies of surprisal have used such language models (e.g. Hale, 2001; Levy, 2008; Demberg & Keller, 2008; Mitchell et al., 2010; Monsalve et al., 2012).

Unfortunately, however, computational language models are still substantially worse than humans at predicting upcoming words, meaning there is some mismatch between the probabilities $p(w|c)$ being estimated computationally and the implicit probabilities in the brains of readers that humans are using. This situation raises the question of to what extent we can trust results about the effects of surprisal as estimated by such language models. To try to get some information about possible biases that might exist in our results based on language models being worse than humans at

Proceedings of the 8th Workshop on Cognitive Modeling and Computational Linguistics (CMCL 2018), pages 10–18,
Salt Lake City, Utah, USA, January 7, 2018. ©2018 Association for Computational Linguistics

predicting upcoming words, poor *linguistic quality*, we can compare a range of computational language models of varying linguistic quality and see how the estimated effects of surprisal change. If there is a trend in results as the linguistic quality of the language models improves, that would provide evidence that such a trend may be even more present in language models with human-level linguistic quality.

Additionally, recent years have seen rapid progress in computational language modeling, enabled by recent advances in neural networks. As a result, the linguistic quality of contemporary language models is far beyond what has been used in previous work studying surprisal. In this paper, we address both these concerns by analyzing how the predictive power of these surprisal estimates, their *psychological quality*, varies as a function of language model linguistic quality and type.

There has also been substantial interest in the *shape* of the effects of surprisal on reading times, because of theories that predict it to be linear (Levy, 2008; Smith & Levy, 2013; Bicknell & Levy, 2010). A secondary goal of this work is to investigate whether the shape of this effect depends on language model quality or type.

In particular, we compare surprisal estimates using a range of language models of varying linguistic qualities and types, from the n-gram models that have been used in most previous work on surprisal to state-of-the-art LSTM and interpolated-LSTM models. We assess the predictive ability and the size and shape of surprisals derived from each language model using generalized additive mixed-effects models (Wood, 2017) fit to a corpus of eye movements in reading.

The plan for the remainder of this paper is as follows. Section 2 introduces the set of language models we compare and establishes the linguistic quality of each. Then, in Section 3 we quantify the ability of surprisals derived from each language model to predict reading times and see the extent to which this changes with language model type and quality, assuming that effects of surprisal on reading times are linear. In Section 4 we do the same but allow surprisal to have non-linear effects, and we additionally use the non-linear models to assess whether there is evidence that the shape of the surprisal effect changes with language model type or quality. Finally, Section 5 concludes.

2 Language Models

2.1 Corpus

The corpus used for language model estimation was the Google One Billion Word Benchmark (Chelba et al., 2013), hereafter referred to as the "1b corpus". The text data was obtained from news periodicals (similar to the Dundee corpus used for eye-tracking data below). The final corpus contained approximately 0.8 billion words with a vocabulary size of about 800,000.

Although the Dundee Corpus (Kennedy et al., 2003) tokenized entire words with punctuation, our models were trained using separate punctuation as well separated possessives (e.g. *Bill's* $\rightarrow$ [*Bill* , *'s*]). Contractions were tokenized into their constituent full-form words, although contractions were counted as a single word when utilizing word count in e.g. perplexity calculations. These calculations can be seen in Table 1.

2.2 Model types

We compare seven language models of three types: four n-gram models, one LSTM, and two interpolations.

2.2.1 n-gram

The n-gram, count-based models were calculated using `kenlm` (Heafield et al., 2013). `kenlm` uses Modified Kneser-Ney Smoothing, and is similar in functionality but significantly faster than SRILM (Stolcke et al., 2011). We calculated 5-grams, 4-grams, trigram, bigrams and unigrams. Unigram results were not included in the study, but rather used as a count of word frequency for controlling other models.

2.2.2 LSTM

Neural network-based language models were generated from a Recurrent Neural Network (RNN) with Long-Short Term Memory (LSTM). Each word was encoded as a 50-dimensional one-hot vector, This vector was then fed into a sequence model with an LSTM of 50 hidden units. The model did not evaluate character-level sequences, but rather only word-level sequences. The probability of the next word in the sequence was selected from the output layer of the sequence model.

2.2.3 Interpolation

In addition to the LSTM and n-gram models, two interpolated models were also built from the two models with the lowest perplexity on the Dundee Corpus used in this study (see Table 1). This was similar to the interpolation method utilized in Jozefowicz et al. (2016). Similar to Jozefowicz et al. (2016), the present study also found optimal weightings for combining an LSTM model with a smoothed n-gram model. Optimal weighting was operationalized as the blend weights that resulted in the lowest perplexity. Perplexity of the interpolated LSTM+5=gram model was optimal (lowest) when an interpolated model weighted the LSTM probabilities by 0.71, with the 5-gram model weighted by 0.29. In addition to this optimal model, a balanced interpolated model was also constructed using equal weighting of the LSTM and 5-gram probabilities.

2.3 Dundee corpus surprisals

The Dundee Corpus (see Section 3 for corpus details) was tokenized at the word (rather than token) level with leading, trailing and internal punctuation included, e.g. *Bill's, couldn't* or *exist!*. Because the 1b Corpus was tokenized, we were required to break words made up of multiple tokens into their constituent parts. The surprisal (log probability) for each token was matched to the 1b Corpus surprisals. In order to realign the tokens with the Dundee Corpus's words, the log probabilities of each constituent token were added together to form a sum total log probability of the word.

Of the approximately 61,000 tokens in the Dundee Corpus, 175 were OOV in the 1b Corpus. These OOV words were removed from the final analysis. In adition, although the 1b Corpus used the sentence-final delimiter </s>, the Dundee Corpus did not. Therefore, while sentence-final delimiters were used in constructing the probabilities of the respective language models, they were also removed from the final analysis.

2.4 Perplexity

For each language model, the words' surprisals (log probabilities) were summed and normalized by the word count. The exponent of the inverse of this sum was then calculated. A lower perplexity is indicative of a more accurate language model. For example, a perplexity of 50 means that the model can guess 1 of 50 different options for the model with equal probability. Therefore a lower perplexity means that there are fewer equally likely model options. The perplexity of the seven language models is laid out in Table 1. The

Language Model	Perplexity (All Tokens)	Perplexity (Excluding OOV)
Interpolated-Optimal	73.39	73.41
Interpolated-Balanced	76.39	76.36
LSTM	113.27	113.59
5-gram	168.98	161.43
4-gram	172.24	164.56
3-gram	191.13	182.65
2-gram	290.88	278.36

Table 1: Perplexity of language models generated either as a LSTM, n-grams, or an interpolation of both the LSTM model as well as the 5-gram model. Perplexities were calculated for the entire Dundee corpus ($60,916$ tokens) as well as for only the tokens in the 1b corpus ($60,741$ tokens).

optimal interpolated model achieved the lowest perplexity, while the bigram model had the worst (highest) perplexity.

It should be noted that the perplexities of both the optimal interpolated model (73) and the LSTM model (113) are worse than the respective models reported in Jozefowicz et al. (2016) and Chelba et al. (2013). Whereas our best 5-gram model achieves a perplexity of 169 on the Dundee corpus, Jozefowicz et al. (2016) achieves a perplexity of 67 on the lm_1b benchmark using a similar model. However, an important distinction is that the perplexities in Table 1 were calculated after all unknown words were excluded. On the other hand, Chelba et al. (2013) used an <UNK> token for words that were OOV on the test portion of the 1b Corpus. This suggests a substantial mismatch between the test benchmark corpus and the Dundee corpus, even though both corpora are sourced from news media. Nonetheless, both perplexity figures could be considered strong, low perplexities.

3 Linear effects of surprisal

In this section we investigate the ability of surprisals derived from each of these seven language models described above to predict reading times in a large corpus of eye movements in reading.

3.1 Methods

3.1.1 Eye movement in reading data

The eye tracking data for our study came from English portion of the Dundee Corpus (Kennedy et al., 2003), which recorded the eye-movement data from 10 English-speaking participants reading newspaper editorials in *The Independent*. For this paper specifically, we predict gaze durations for each word, defined to be the sum of all fixations made on a word between the time the word is initially fixed and when the eyes first move off of the word. This measure is only calculated if the word is fixated by that reader prior to any fixation on a later word (i.e., during 'first pass' reading). If the word was not fixated during first pass reading, this is missing data. We used a total of about 436,000 valid gaze durations in the English portion of the Dundee corpus. After performing the exclusions listed below, we were left with a total of 289,726 gaze durations and a vocabulary size of 37,420 word types.

In line with previous studies of gaze durations in the Dundee corpus (e.g. Smith & Levy, 2013), we excluded:

- Words preceding punctuation
- Words with non-alphabetical characters
- Words that were presented to participants at the beginning or end of a line of text
- Words that were outside the vocabulary of the 1b corpus (and thus the language models)

Because our statistical model of the gaze duration of each word also included effects of the surprisal of the preceding word, we also excluded:

- Words following punctuation
- Words that followed words with non-alphabetic characters
- Words that followed words that were outside the vocabulary of the 1b corpus (and thus the language models)

3.1.2 Statistical models

Similar to Smith & Levy (2013), we used generalized additive mixed-effects models (GAMMs) to predict reading times with the `mgcv` (Wood, 2004) package in R (R Core Team, 2013). We estimated seven GAMMs, one for each language model. Each GAMM modeled gaze duration on a word as a function of two linear surprisal terms: one for the surprisal of the current word and one for the surprisal of the previous word. Each GAMM also included random intercepts for each of the 10 readers and a range of linear and non-linear covariates not of direct interest for the present work, identical to those included by Smith & Levy (2013). These covariates were:

- a tensor product interaction between orthographic word length and log-frequency (unigram log probability estimated from the 1b corpus) of the current word
- a tensor product interaction between orthographic word length and log-frequency of the previous word
- a spline effect of word number within the text
- a binary variable of whether or not the previous word had received a fixation

3.1.3 Analysis

We compare the predictive power of different language models for reading times by comparing the log likelihoods across GAMMs that include surprisals derived from different language models.[1] To enable comparison of log likelihoods across models, we change two aspects of mgcv's default GAMM fitting procedure: we use maximum likelihood fitting instead of REML and we use splines with fixed degrees of freedom instead of penalized splines. We set the fixed degrees of freedom for each covariate to be a bit above the estimated degrees of freedom from a GAMM estimated in the default way (which was relatively constant across models).

To measure the added predictive power of the two linear surprisal terms in each model, we subtract the models' log likelihood from a model that only includes the covariates, yielding a measure we denote ΔLogLik. (Note that because these models are in a subset relationship -2 times ΔLogLik is a Chi-square distributed deviance as in a likelihood ratio test.)

To assess the extent to which this measure of predictive power is related to the language model's linguistic quality, we correlate this ΔLogLik metric with perplexity. Additionally, since these models with linear effects of surprisal also estimate the coefficient of surprisal for predicting reading times – both for the current word's surprisal and the prior word's – we also assess the correlation between these coefficients and the model's perplexity. To the extent to which there are systematic relationships between these coefficients and the language model's linguistic quality, it may suggest that poor

---

[1]Technically, these models include $\log_{10}$ probabilities, which must be multiplied by -1 to get a surprisal, and also converted from bans to bits.

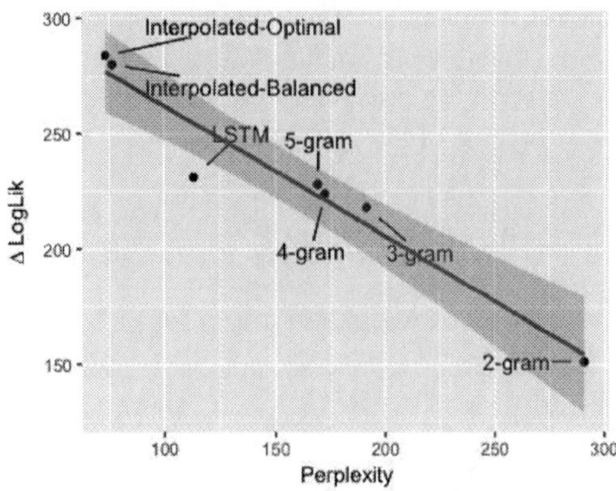

Figure 1: Improvements in log likelihood for linear models, charted against decreases in perplexity. Distance from the central trend line is indicative of larger departures in log likelihood as a function of perplexity. The blue line represents a linear best fit, with a coefficient of -1.66 and $R^2 = 0.94$

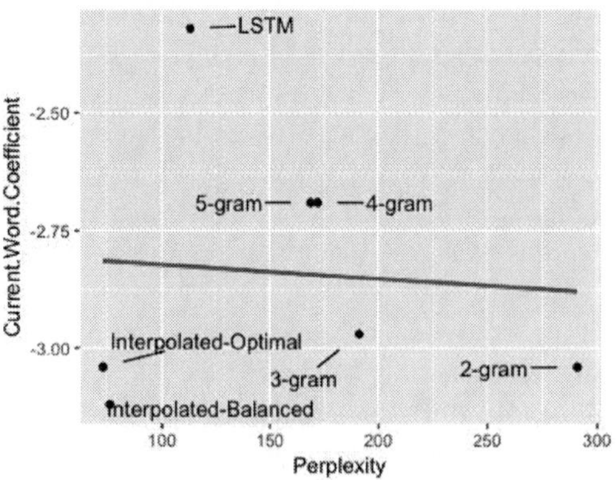

Figure 2: Changes in the current word's coefficient for linear models, charted against increases in perplexity. Distances from the central trend line are indicative of larger departures of the current word coefficient from the expected trend. Regardless of perplexity, the coefficient is stable. The blue line represents a linear best fit, with a coefficient of -2.79 and $R^2 = 0.007$.

quality language models cannot be trusted to accurately estimate the size of the effect of surprisal on reading times.

3.2 Results and discussion

3.2.1 Log Likelihood

As shown in Figure 1 and Table 2, there is a monotonic effect of language model quality on predictive power. Better language models (lower perplexity) yield surprisal values that better predict reading times, as seen by increased ΔLogLik. Indeed, Figure 1 shows a strikingly strong relationship between a language model's linguistic quality (measured by perplexity) and the ability of surprisal values derived from that model to predict reading times (measured by ΔLogLik). These two values have an R^2 of 0.94.

However, there is one relatively clear departure from this tight linear relationship. Namely, the large decrease in the perplexity going from the 5-gram model to the LSTM is not reflected in a large jump in ΔLogLik. Put another way, although there is a clear systematic relationship between language model linguistic *quality* and ΔLogLik, there is also some evidence for effects of language model *type*, such that the LSTM is less useful for predicting reading times than would be expected given its perplexity.

3.2.2 Current Word

The effects of two words' surprisal was incorporated into the GAMs: the surprisal of the current word and the surprisal of the previous word. Despite the different models' very different perplexities, the *size* of the effects of surprisal were estimated very stably across language models. As seen in Figure 2, all models had surprisal coefficients around 3 (although the LSTM model is again somewhat of a low outlier). There is no clear relationship between the coefficients for the surprisal of the current word and language model quality, with both the best model (optimal interpolation) and the worst model (bigrams) having a value of 3.04.

3.2.3 Previous Word

Similar to the results above for the current word, the previous word's surprisal also had an inconsistent effect across models. In other words, the coefficient for the previous word's surprisal (see Table 2) bore no clear relationship with relative improvements in language model perplexity.

4 Non-linear effects of surprisal

In addition to the previous set of analyses analyzing the predictive power of *linear* effects of surprisal on reading times, we conducted another set of analyses allowing for non-linear effects of sur-

Language Model	ΔLogLik	Current Word Coefficient	Previous Word Coefficient
Interpolated-Optimal	284	-3.04	-4.57
Interpolated-Balanced	280	-3.12	-4.68
LSTM	231	-2.32	-2.56
5-gram	228	-2.69	-3.82
4-gram	224	-2.69	-3.81
3-gram	218	-2.97	-3.92
2-gram	151	-3.04	-3.98

Table 2: As the perplexity of a language model increases, its improvement over baseline log likelihood (ΔLogLik) decreases. The coefficients for both the current and previous words do not bear a consistent relationship with model perplexity.

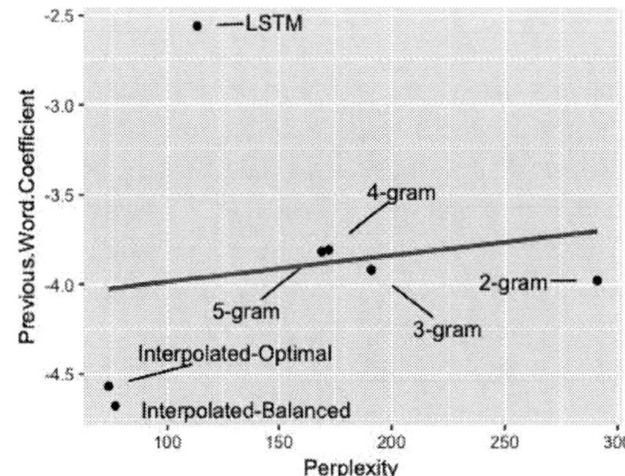

Figure 3: Regression plot of coefficients on the previous word. The blue line represents a linear best fit, with a coefficient of 0.001 and $R^2 = 0.03$.

	R^2	p
Linear		
Log Likelihood	0.94	0.0003
Current Word Coefficient	0.01	0.86
Previous Word Coefficient	0.03	0.73
Non-Linear		
Log Likelihood	0.98	0.00002
Current Word F	0.25	0.26
Previous Word F	0.99	0.000008

Table 3: Correlation results for metrics of predictors of linear and non-linear GAMMs

prisal. These models also let us ask whether the *shape* of the estimated effect of surprisal on reading times varies with language model quality.

4.1 Methodology

The primary methodology was identical to that from the previous analysis, except that instead of including linear effects of current and previous word surprisal in the GAMMs, we included cubic splines (40 d.f.) of current and previous word surprisal. For this non-linear model, since there are not coefficients of current and previous word surprisal, we also investigate the F statistic associated with the strength of each surprisal term predictor.

Additionally, to analyze whether the *shape* of the surprisal effect differs across conditions, we fit additional GAMMs that had the same structure but were estimated in mgcv's usual way (i.e., with splines penalized and REML). These addi-

tional models were only used for visualization.

4.2 Results and discussion

When allowing for non-linear effects of surprisal, the relationship between linguistic quality and predictive power for reading times becomes even more clear. The relationship between ΔLogLik and perplexity becomes even stronger (Figure 4), with an R^2 of 0.98. Further, as seen in Table 4, while the F statistic for the current word surprisal is inconsistent as model perplexity improves (similar to the coefficients of surprisal in the linear models), the F statistic of the *previous* word is tightly related to perplexity. As perplexity of a model improves, the F statistic of the previous word improves in lockstep. This suggests that at least in the non-linear models, many of the improvements in predictive ability may come specifically from effects of prior word surprisal.

As can be seen in the GAM plots in Figures 5 and 6, there are no large differences in the shape

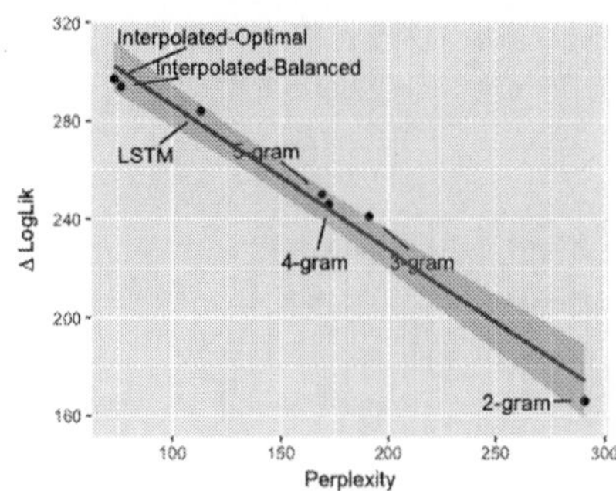

Figure 4: Improvements in log likelihood for non-linear models, charted against decreases in perplexity. The blue line is a linear best fit line with a coefficient of -1.66, $R^2 = 0.98$.

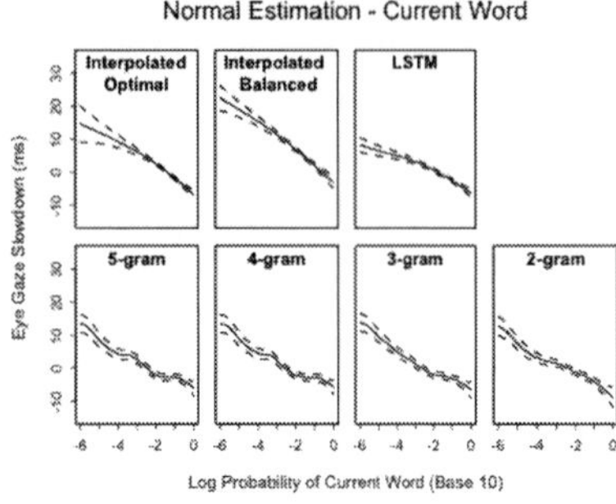

Figure 5: GAM plots on current word using normal estimation

of surprisal as language model quality improves – all look roughly linear. If a trend in shape does exist, the highest quality models (interpolation) appear to have the most linear slopes. Additionally, the slope for surprisal of the prior word appears to flatten out for LSTMs for high surprisals.[2]

5   General Discussion

Taking all of the results together, we have shown evidence here for a strong effect of language model linguistic quality on the predictive power of surprisals estimated from that language model for reading times. This effect holds regardless of whether surprisal is modeled as a linear or non-linear effect. Despite this clear relationship with linguistic quality in terms of predictive power, we also saw remarkable consistency. Across language

---

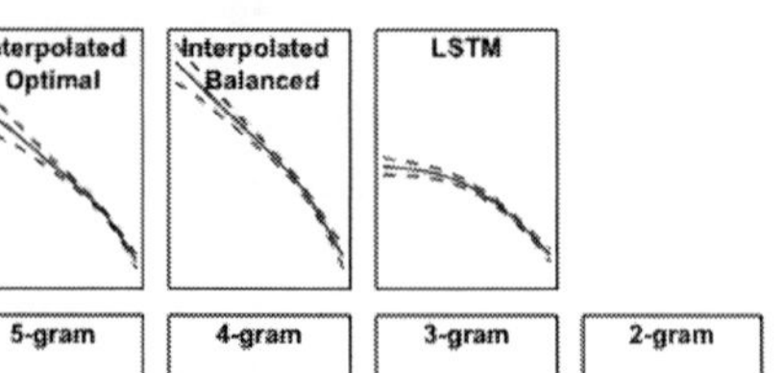

Figure 6: GAM plots on previous word using normal estimation

models that varied by more than a factor of 4 in perplexity, the size of the effect of surprisal was estimated to be the similar and the shape of the effect of surprisal was estimated to be roughly linear. These results suggest that we can put a reasonable amount of trust in results about surprisal estimated with computational language models, despite the state-of-the-art still being far from human quality.

In addition, the way that the language models were composed seems to play a role in its fit to the data. The LSTM-based model does seem to be somewhat of a low-performing outlier. However, when the LSTM model is used with the 5-gram model in interpolation, these yield superior results. Therefore, although a purely LSTM-based model does not predict reading time as well as other models, it provides a good fit for the data. When used in conjunction with a count-based model, this combination provides more accurate predictions of the reading time data.

A number of studies have used the Dundee eye-tracking corpus in conjunction with a probabilistic language model. Demberg & Keller (2008), using less sophisticated linear models, found that surprisal is an accurate measure of processing complexity as measured by eye gaze duration. According to Demberg & Keller (2008), greater word surprisal invokes higher "integration costs," which accounts for prolonged gaze duration.

In a neural network language model, word dependencies can span an arbitrary word distance, i.e. not all dependencies are contingent upon adjacent words or even a neighboring word. For example, ellipsis can span multiple clause boundaries to resolve an anaphoric relationship. For this

---

[2]This approach was followed rather than performing a statistical model comparison testing for non-linearity because our GAMM models lacked by-word random slopes. Because the model lacks these parameters, we would expect the model to capture variance across word tokens in the corpus by bending the curve away from linearity.

Language Model	ΔLogLik	Current Word F Statistic	Previous Word F Statistic
Interpolated-Optimal	297	21.13	63.8
Interpolated-Balanced	294	21.76	63.27
LSTM	284	17.58	55.16
5-gram	250	21.31	50.47
4-gram	246	21.18	50.13
3-gram	241	22.86	48.12
2-gram	166	15.6	34.94

Table 4: Log likelihood and F statistics for GAMMs with nonlinear smoothers on all covariates

reason, surprisal that accounts for the hierarchical structure of language has also been studied, to see if taking hierarchy into account can better predict eye gaze duration. Frank & Bod (2011) concludes that including hierarchy information does not better account for variance compared to a sequence-based model. According to their study, hierarchical information does not noticeably affect the generation of expectations of the following word.

Fossum & Levy (2012), on the other hand, make various modifications to the models used in Frank & Bod (2011), adding additional lexical information to the unlexicalized hierarchical models. Fossum & Levy (2012) concludes that hierarchical information, when properly lexicalized, can improve sequence-only lexical models. Similarly, Mitchell et al. (2010) created a model that interpolates syntactic and distributional semantic information, and found that this improved the prediction of eye tracking durations.

As this bears on the present study, the LSTM model is able to detect word relationships that span arbitrary distances. While the LSTM model is not explicitly representing hierarchical information, the model does capture long distance information. Our results show that the LSTM model outperforms the purely n-gram models in terms of predictive capabilities. Thus, while we do not need to build hierarchical information explicitly into our model, the long-distance information does improve both linguistic and psychological accuracy. This could point to the conclusion that eye gaze duration is also sensitive to, if not hierarchical information, then information provided at a long distance from the current word.

In a similar vein to our results, Monsalve et al. (2012) shows that perplexity of a language model (linguistic accuracy) bears a strong relationship to the log likelihood of a reading time model (psy-chological accuracy). The key differences between this study and ours is that Monsalve et al. (2012) analyzes self-paced reading data rather than eye-tracking, and that we use higher-performing state-of-the-art language models.

Finally, the present study can, in many respects, be viewed as a follow-up to Smith & Levy (2013). (Smith & Levy, 2013) measured the shape of the surprisal curve, similar to our experiment in Section 4; however, the present study demonstrates that the the effect of surprisal is still linear even with much more (linguistically and psychologically) accurate language models.

As many studies have noted (Monsalve et al., 2012; Frank et al., 2013), a corpus such as the Dundee corpus, collected from newspapers, often requires a great deal of global, extra-sentential context. Therefore, when processing a given sentence, the reader must also take into account information provided many sentences prior, or even not provided in the document at all. This limitation could impact the results reported herein.

Despite possible limitations, the results above provide consistent evidence that improving the linguistic accuracy of language models will improve the models' ability to make psychological predictions. This underscores the importance of understanding language structure in order to better understand cognitive processes such as eye gaze duration.

Acknowledgements

We wish to thank Tal Linzen for providing code for interfacing with Google's lm_1b LSTM language model. This research was supported by NSF Award 1734217 (Bicknell)

References

Bicknell, K., & Levy, R. (2010). A rational model of eye movement control in reading. In J. Hajivc, S. Carberry, S. Clark, & J. Nivre (Eds.), *Proceedings of the 48th annual meeting of the association for computational linguistics (acl)* (pp. 1168–1178). Uppsala, Sweden: Association for Computational Linguistics.

Chelba, C., Mikolov, T., Schuster, M., Ge, Q., Brants, T., Koehn, P., & Robinson, T. (2013). One billion word benchmark for measuring progress in statistical language modeling. *arXiv preprint arXiv:1312.3005.*

Demberg, V., & Keller, F. (2008). Data from eye-tracking corpora as evidence for theories of syntactic processing complexity. *Cognition, 109*(2), 193–210.

Fossum, V., & Levy, R. (2012). Sequential vs. hierarchical syntactic models of human incremental sentence processing. In *Proceedings of the 3rd workshop on cognitive modeling and computational linguistics* (pp. 61–69).

Frank, S. L., & Bod, R. (2011). Insensitivity of the human sentence-processing system to hierarchical structure. *Psychological science, 22*(6), 829–834.

Frank, S. L., Monsalve, I. F., Thompson, R. L., & Vigliocco, G. (2013). Reading time data for evaluating broad-coverage models of english sentence processing. *Behavior Research Methods, 45*(4), 1182–1190.

Hale, J. (2001). A probabilistic Earley parser as a psycholinguistic model. In *Proceedings of the second meeting of the north american chapter of the association for computational linguistics on language technologies* (pp. 1–8).

Heafield, K., Pouzyrevsky, I., Clark, J. H., & Koehn, P. (2013, August). Scalable modified Kneser-Ney language model estimation. In *Proceedings of the 51st annual meeting of the association for computational linguistics* (pp. 690–696). Sofia, Bulgaria. Retrieved from `https://kheafield.com/papers/edinburgh/estimate_paper.pdf`

Jozefowicz, R., Vinyals, O., Schuster, M., Shazeer, N., & Wu, Y. (2016). Exploring the limits of language modeling. *arXiv preprint arXiv:1602.02410.*

Kennedy, A., Hill, R., & Pynte, J. (2003). The dundee corpus. In *Proceedings of the 12th european conference on eye movement.*

Levy, R. (2008). Expectation-based syntactic comprehension. *Cognition, 106*(3), 1126–1177.

Mitchell, J., Lapata, M., Demberg, V., & Keller, F. (2010). Syntactic and semantic factors in processing difficulty: An integrated measure. In *Proceedings of the 48th annual meeting of the association for computational linguistics* (pp. 196–206).

Monsalve, I. F., Frank, S. L., & Vigliocco, G. (2012). Lexical surprisal as a general predictor of reading time. In *Proceedings of the 13th conference of the european chapter of the association for computational linguistics* (pp. 398–408).

R Core Team. (2013). R: A language and environment for statistical computing [Computer software manual]. Vienna, Austria. Retrieved from `http://www.R-project.org/`

Shannon, C. E. (1948). A mathematical theory of communication. *Bell System Technical Journal, 27*(3), 379–423. Retrieved from `http://dx.doi.org/10.1002/j.1538-7305.1948.tb01338.x` doi: 10.1002/j.1538-7305.1948.tb01338.x

Smith, N., & Levy, R. (2011). Cloze but no cigar: The complex relationship between cloze, corpus, and subjective probabilities in language processing. In *Proceedings of the cognitive science society* (Vol. 33).

Smith, N., & Levy, R. (2013). The effect of word predictability on reading time is logarithmic. *Cognition, 128*(3), 302–319.

Stolcke, A., Zheng, J., Wang, W., & Abrash, V. (2011). Srilm at sixteen: Update and outlook. In *Proceedings of ieee automatic speech recognition and understanding workshop* (Vol. 5).

Taylor, W. L. (1953). " Cloze procedure": a new tool for measuring readability. *Journalism quarterly.*

Wood, S. N. (2004). Stable and efficient multiple smoothing parameter estimation for generalized additive models. *Journal of the American Statistical Association, 99*(467), 673-686.

Wood, S. N. (2017). *Generalized additive models: An introduction with R* (2nd ed.). Chapman and Hall/CRC.

Dynamic encoding of structural uncertainty in gradient symbols

Pyeong Whan Cho
Department of Cognitive Science
Johns Hopkins University
pcho4@jhu.edu

Matthew Goldrick
Department of Linguistics
Northwestern University
matt-goldrick@northwestern.edu

Richard L. Lewis
Department of Psychology
University of Michigan
rickl@umich.edu

Paul Smolensky
Department of Cognitive Science
Johns Hopkins University
smolensky@jhu.edu

Abstract

An important achievement in modeling online language comprehension is the discovery of the relationship between processing difficulty and surprisal (Hale, 2001; Levy, 2008). However, it is not clear how structural uncertainty can be represented and updated in a continuous-time continuous-state dynamical system model, a reasonable abstraction of neural computation. In this study, we investigate the Gradient Symbolic Computation (GSC) model (Smolensky et al., 2014) and show how it can dynamically encode and update structural uncertainty via the gradient activation of symbolic constituents. We claim that surprisal is closely related to the amount of change in the optimal activation state driven by a new word input. In a simulation study, we demonstrate that the GSC model implementing a simple probabilistic symbolic grammar can simulate the effect of surprisal on processing time. Our model provides a mechanistic account of the effect of surprisal, bridging between probabilistic symbolic models and subsymbolic connectionist models.

1 Introduction

A core computational problem in online language comprehension is to deal with local ambiguity, the one-to-many mapping from a unit symbol w_k (e.g., word) to symbol strings containing w at the k-th position $W_k^* = \cdots w_k \cdots$ and their interpretations S (e.g., sentences and their parses). Rational models of sentence comprehension solve this problem by computing $P(S|W_k)$, a conditional probability of interpretations given a partial string of symbols (henceforth, prefix) $W_k = w_1 \cdots w_k$,

and updating it discretely for every new symbol input (Jurafsky, 1996; Hale, 2001; Levy, 2008). We will refer to this class of incremental processing models simply as (structural) probabilistic models.

The probabilistic model has drawn a lot of attention because it predicts processing difficulty in different regions of a sentence based on information-theoretic complexity metrics. The surprisal hypothesis (e.g., Hale, 2001; Levy, 2008) claims that reading time of w_k (as a measure of processing difficulty) is proportional to its surprisal, $-\log P(w_k|W_{k-1})$, or equivalently, the Kullback-Leibler (KL) divergence of $P(S|W_k)$ from $P(S|W_{k-1})$ (Levy, 2008). This hypothesis has been supported in many psycholinguistic experiments (e.g., Boston et al., 2008; Demberg and Keller, 2008; Smith and Levy, 2013).

In this study, our goal is to provide a neurally-plausible, mechanistic account of the relationship between surprisal and processing time. For our purpose, we need a model from which both kinds of information, $P(S|W_k)$ and processing times of w_k, can be collected directly without relying on stipulated linking hypotheses. Since the model is a dynamical system, processing time is directly modeled. To model the probability $P(S|W_k)$ relevant for rational analysis, we treat the model, primarily developed to study interpretation, as a *generator*: it is run to equilibrium with no input, producing a sentence parse as output. This is done repeatedly as the dynamical system is stochastic; this gives a probability distribution over generated parses we call $^*P(S)$: this we take to be the knowledge of sentence probabilities that is embodied in the model's dynamics. Then for any W_k, for rational analysis we compute $^*P(S|W_k)$ by conditioning $^*P(S)$ on W_k, i.e., $^*P(S|W_k)$ is the proportion of all generated parses that have prefix equal to W_k. We can then examine the extent to which the model, when serving as an incremental

19

Proceedings of the 8th Workshop on Cognitive Modeling and Computational Linguistics (CMCL 2018), pages 19–28,
Salt Lake City, Utah, USA, January 7, 2018. ©2018 Association for Computational Linguistics

parser, behaves in accord with rational inference given its knowledge.

The Gradient Symbolic Computation (GSC) framework (Smolensky et al., 2014) serves our goal. The GSC model is a continuous-time, continuous-state stochastic dynamical system model that computes the representation of a discrete structure gradually. This framework grew out of the Integrated Connectionist/Symbolic cognitive architecture (Smolensky and Legendre, 2006). GSC aims to provide an integrated account of the contribution of the continuous dynamics of cognitive processing and the discrete competence that characterizes our knowledge of language.

Cho et al. (2017) applied the framework to incremental processing problems focusing on transient dynamics during incremental processing and argued that the model can achieve two core computational goals in incremental processing: maintaining multiple context-appropriate and globally-coherent interpretations while rejecting interpretations that are context-inappropriate. The GSC parser meets these challenges by moving, during the processing of a word, to an intermediate activation state (a *blend state*) in which multiple symbolic constituents are simultaneously activated to varying partial degrees. From this state, the parser can reach all activation states representing context-appropriate and globally-coherent structures but does not move to activation states representing context-inappropriate structures (either grammatical or ungrammatical). The relation between intermediate activation states and probability distributions over discrete parses was briefly discussed but was not investigated systematically.

In this study, we propose a version of the GSC parser and show how it can be related to other probabilistic sentence-processing models. We argue that the parser's internal state – the activation values of multiple symbolic constituents along with control parameters of the parser – encodes a probability distribution over complete parses (Section 3). After encountering new input, the parser incrementally changes its internal state to encode a new probability distribution. The work the parser needs to do to shift this internal state is closely related to the KL divergence between the probability distributions, providing a link between processing time and surprisal (Section 4). In a simulation study (Section 5), we demonstrate that the GSC parser can approximate rational inference and re-

port the correlation between processing time and surprisal in our model. In Section 6, we summarize our results and discuss some implications of our work.

2   Gradient Symbolic Computation

2.1   Representation

Consider a tree structure $\texttt{S[1](A,B)}$.[1] Let us assign a unique label for every position (called *role*) in the tree structure. For example, we assign labels $\texttt{r}, \texttt{0}, \texttt{1}$ to the mother (root) and the left and right daughter nodes, respectively. Then, we can describe the tree as an unordered set of symbol/position (or *filler/role*) bindings: $\texttt{S[1](A,B)} \equiv \{\texttt{B/1}, \texttt{S[1]/r}, \texttt{A/0}\}$.

Let $\mathbf{f}$ and $\mathbf{r}$ be subsymbolic vector encodings of filler $\texttt{f}$ and role $\texttt{r}$. The encoding of binding $\texttt{f/r}$ is defined as the tensor product of the two vectors: $\texttt{f/r} \equiv \mathbf{f} \otimes \mathbf{r}$ whose (i,j)-th component is the product of the i-th component of $\mathbf{f}$ and the j-th component of $\mathbf{r}$. The encoding of a set of filler/role bindings is defined as the superposition (vector sum) of the encodings of component bindings: $\{\texttt{f}_1/\texttt{r}_1, \cdots, \texttt{f}_k/\texttt{r}_k\} \equiv \sum_k \mathbf{f_k} \otimes \mathbf{r_k}$. For example, $\texttt{S[1](A,B)} \equiv \mathbf{S[1]} \otimes \mathbf{r} + \mathbf{A} \otimes \mathbf{0} + \mathbf{B} \otimes \mathbf{1}$.

In this study, we used local representation (or one-hot encodings) of fillers and roles for facilitating computation. However, many equivalent models with distributed representations can be easily constructed by change of basis (Smolensky, 1986). The result will not change if the distributed representations of bindings remain orthonormal (Smolensky, 1990).

2.2   Constraints

The GSC model uses Harmonic Grammar (HG) (Hale and Smolensky, 2006) to specify grammars via *soft constraints* each of which imposes a reward (a 'positive constraint') or a penalty (a 'negative constraint') on the wellformedness or *Grammatical Harmony* of a gradient symbolic structure. The grammatical structures are those with maximal grammatical Harmony: these structures best satisfy the constraints of the grammar.

As an example, consider a rewrite rule: $\texttt{S[1]} \rightarrow \texttt{A B}$. This rule defines a treelet $\texttt{S[1](A,B)}$ as

---

[1] The motivation of using bracketed symbols (e.g., $\texttt{S[1]}$) is presented in Hale and Smolensky (2006). For our purpose, it suffices to say that a bracketed symbol can be considered as a different instance of the same class which has a unique pair of children.

grammatical. HG assigns a positive Harmony reward to any structure for every grammatical pair of bindings — e.g., $(\text{S}[1]/\text{r}, \text{A}/0)$ — it contains. In a network implementation of this HG, these binary rules are implemented as positive weights on between-binding connections, so that whenever one binding is active, it sends positive activation to its grammatical parent and child binding(s).

In addition to these positive contributions from grammatical mother/daughter pairs, the Harmonic Grammar assigns a negative penalty $-b$ to every filler, where b is the number of edges that the filler must have in a grammatical structure. If all those edges are grammatically legal, they will produce positive binary rewards which by design exactly cancel the unary penalties, so that an illformed tree has negative Harmony but a wellformed tree has zero Harmony — the maximum value. The unary HG rules are implemented as negative weights on self-connections of binding units.

The Grammatical Harmony of a set of active filler/role bindings is simply the sum of the Harmony values assigned by all binary and unary HG rules. In the GSC implementation, Grammatical Harmony is defined as in Eq. 1.

$$H_G(\mathbf{a}; \mathbf{W}, \mathbf{ex}) = \frac{1}{2}\mathbf{a}^\top \mathbf{W}\mathbf{a} + \mathbf{ex}^\top \mathbf{a} \qquad (1)$$

where $\mathbf{a}$ is an activation state vector, $\mathbf{W}$ is a weight matrix implementing the grammatical constraints, and $\mathbf{ex}$ is an external input vector, stimulating the target terminal binding corresponding to the present input word. For example, suppose the model is given a second word 'B'. Because it is the second word of a sentence, it must occupy the second terminal role (in our case, 1).[2] Thus, the component of $\mathbf{ex}$ corresponding to binding $\text{B}/1$ has a positive value (a model parameter) and all the other components have a value of 0.

The goal of the GSC parser is to produce an output that represents a discrete tree (at least to a good approximation). This turns out to require further constraints which penalize representations that are not approximately discrete. The Harmony term in Eq. 2, in which f and r are filler and role indices, penalizes representations with multiple symbols filling the same role: it introduces competition among bindings in each role. It is called the *Competition Constraint*. The Harmony term in Eq. 3

penalizes every binding whose activation value is not close to either 0 or 1 — this is the crucial *Discreteness Constraint*, and H_Q is *Discreteness Harmony*. Note that the Competition and Discreteness Constraints in collaboration force the model to choose one filler, with activation 1, in each role. The representations of discrete trees satisfy both these constraints[3] and fall on what we call the *grid* of states: in these states, for each role, the bindings of that role to all symbols all have activation 0 except one, which has activation 1. The representation of the tree $\text{S}[1]\,[\text{A B}]$ is on the grid, while an example non-grid state is the one encoding $0.3\,\text{S}[1]\,[(0.2\,\text{A} + 0.5\,\text{C})\,(0.4\,\text{B} - 0.1\,\text{D})]$

Finally, to ensure the network state does not blow up, we also impose the Baseline Constraint (Eq. 4), which penalizes activation state distant from a baseline activation state $\mathbf{z}$.

$$H_C(\mathbf{a}) = -\sum_r \left(1 - \sum_f a_{f,r}^2\right)^2 \qquad (2)$$

$$H_Q(\mathbf{a}) = -\sum_r \sum_f (a_{f,r})^2 (1 - a_{f,r})^2 \qquad (3)$$

$$H_B(\mathbf{a}; \mathbf{z}) = -\frac{1}{2}\|\mathbf{a} - \mathbf{z}\|^2 \qquad (4)$$

The Total Harmony H is the weighted sum of the four Harmony values in Equations 1 – 4:

$$H(\mathbf{a}) = H_G(\mathbf{a}) + \beta H_B(\mathbf{a}) + c H_C(\mathbf{a}) + q H_Q(\mathbf{a})$$

where β, c, and q are the coefficients of nongrammatical constraints. While β and c are fixed, q changes in time, controlled by an external mechanism we do not model here.

The coefficient q governs the strength of the constraint to have discrete activation values (0 or 1) — that is, the strength of the requirement that the model *commit* to symbols being predicted to be present or absent. The Competition Constraint prohibits more than one symbol having activation 1 in any given role, so large q values force the model to *choose* among competitors. Hence we refer to q as the *commitment level*.

2.3 Processing dynamics

The model updates its activation state $\mathbf{a}$ as follows:

$$d\mathbf{a} = \nabla_{\mathbf{a}} H(\mathbf{a}; q(t))dt + \sqrt{2T}\,dW \qquad (5)$$

where W is the standard multidimensional Wiener process and T is the level of noise. $\nabla_{\mathbf{a}} H(\mathbf{a})$ is the

---

[2] In this study, we consider minimal tree structures so the three role labels $\text{r}, 0, 1$ will be enough. To deal with deep structures, a more elaborated role labeling system is required.

[3] There is a special Null Symbol "@" which is bound to every role that would otherwise be empty.

gradient of the total harmony evaluated at $\mathbf{a}$. The model optimizes the constraints by stochastically following the gradient, a Brownian motion with drift given by the gradient of Harmony hence, on average, increasing Harmony over time.

$q(t)$ is the commitment level at time t. For convenience, we assume that $q(0) = 0$ and q increases in time because the goal of computation (either in production or in comprehension) is to build a discrete symbolic structure. We will refer to how q changes in time as the *commitment policy* and discuss it in more detail in Section 3.

3 GSC parser as a probabilistic model

3.1 GSC parser

The GSC parser is an application of the GSC framework to incremental parsing. It processes a sentence word-by-word incrementally and passes through intermediate activation states (or blend states) to reach a grid point, the encoding of the parse of the sentence.

Let $\mathbf{ex}_k$, q_k, and $\mathbf{a}_k$ be the external input vector corresponding to w_k, the commitment level and the activation state vector after processing the k-th word. $\mathbf{a}_k$ is a local optimum if $T = 0$. For $T > 0$, we take $\mathbf{a}_k$ to be an approximation of the local optimum. Let $\mathbf{ex}_0 (= \mathbf{0})$, $q_0 (= 0)$, and $\mathbf{a}_0$ be the initial values of the variables before processing the first word of a sentence. As the parser processes a length-N sentence, its activation state changes from $\mathbf{a}_0$ through $\mathbf{a}_k$ to $\mathbf{a}_N$. Taking q_N to be large, $\mathbf{a}_N$ is close to a grid point and is classified into the nearby grid point by choosing the filler most strongly activated in each role (the *snap-to-the-grid* method). Word processing time for w_k is the time the parser takes to move from $\mathbf{a}_{k-1}$ to $\mathbf{a}_k$.

More specifically, the parser processes each word w_k in three phases. Let $\mathbf{a}_k^j$ be the activation state after phase j given word w_k; $\mathbf{a}_k = \mathbf{a}_k^3$.

- Phase 1a: Update $\mathbf{ex}$ from $\mathbf{ex}_{k-1}$ to $\mathbf{ex}_k$.

- Phase 1b: Update $\mathbf{a}$ from $\mathbf{a}_{k-1} (= \mathbf{a}_{k-1}^3)$ to $\mathbf{a}_k^1$, using $H(\mathbf{a}, q_{k-1})$, allowing settling to convergence.

- Phase 2: Update $\mathbf{a}$ from $\mathbf{a}_k^1$ to $\mathbf{a}_k^2$ by using $H(\mathbf{a}, q_{k-1}) \rightarrow H(\mathbf{a}, q_k)$, i.e., increasing from q_{k-1} to q_k at a constant rate $dq/dt = 1$.

- Phase 3: Update $\mathbf{a}$ from $\mathbf{a}_k^2$ to $\mathbf{a}_k^3 (= \mathbf{a}_k)$, using $H(\mathbf{a}, q_k)$, allowing settling to convergence.[4]

The processing time of w_k is defined as the sum of the settling times in phase 1 and 3 and the duration of phase 2.

The parser, in phase 1, integrates a new word input with its internal language model (or structural prediction) and, in phase 2, updates the internal language model via the control of commitment level to make a new structural prediction. In the proposed model, the effect of instantaneous surprisal of w_k (phase 1) is conceptually distinguished from the effect of model update (phase 2) (c.f., O'Reilly et al., 2013).[5]

The role of phase 2 is to reduce the number of grid points reachable from the present activation state.[6] As q increases, the system passes through a series of *bifurcations*, the qualitative changes in the organization of the representation space. When q passes some critical values q_c, more local optima emerge. Each local optimum forms a local hump (*basin of attraction*) on the Harmony surface. Those local optima are separated by Harmony valleys that block transitions from one hump to another: the state seeks higher Harmony. Metaphorically, the paths to some futures (corresponding to different parses) are separated from the present state by these valleys. That is, some structural hypotheses are rejected (Cho and Smolensky, 2016).

Given a length-N sentence, we define a commitment policy π_N as a sequence of q values $(q_0, \cdots, q_k, \cdots, q_N)$ where q_k is the commitment level *after* processing the k-th word in a sentence.

---

[4]During phase 1 and phase 3, the model monitors convergence as follows. Let $H_{max}(t)$ be the maximum total harmony in a phase up through time t. If H_{max} has not been updated for a certain amount of time ($= 0.5$ in our simulation study; Section 5), the phase ends and the following phase begins. During phase 2, q increases at a constant rate $dq/dt = 1$ so the duration of phase 2 is simply $q_k - q_{k-1}$.

[5]Alternatively, we can consider a GSC parser with a discrete commitment policy. Given a new word input w_k, the model updates both q and $\mathbf{ex}$ discretely from q_{k-1} and $\mathbf{ex}_{k-1}$ to q_k and $\mathbf{ex}_k$. Note that the surprisal of w_k is computed given the updated internal model in this alternative model. Although this alternative parsed every sentence of a minimal grammar G (see Section 5) equally well, we prefer the proposed model to the alternative for the following reason. While $\mathbf{ex}_k$ is given from the environment, an optimal value of q_k given $\mathbf{ex}_k$ must be computed by the parser and the computation must take time.

[6]In terms of the number of reachable grid points, entropy is reduced during phase 2. Because the phase-2 duration is a monotonically increasing function of the amount of increase in q and q is associated with entropy (roughly speaking, the higher q, the smaller entropy), it is likely that a longer phase-2 duration is associated with a larger entropy reduction, which is consistent with the entropy reduction hypothesis (Hale, 2006), although the exact relation between q and entropy needs further investigation.

$q_0 = 0$ and q_N is set to q_{max}; in this setting, the model is guaranteed to reach a grid point after processing the whole sentence (to a close approximation; the higher q_{max}, the better the approximation).

3.2 GSC parser as a probabilistic model

The GSC parser can be related to a structural probabilistic model in the following way. Consider a prefix $W_k = w_1 \cdots w_k$ where w_k is not the final word of a sentence. The GSC parser processes the prefix under a policy $\pi_k = (q_0, \cdots, q_k)$. During processing w_k, the activation state changes from $\mathbf{a}_{k-1}$ to $\mathbf{a}_k$. If we set q_k to q_{max}, the parser will be forced to choose a grid point. If $T > 0$ and the same process is run multiple times, the parser will choose different grid points (encodings of S) in different frequencies. In this way, we can estimate a conditional probability that the parser reaches S if it starts from a tuple $(\mathbf{a}_{k-1}, q_{k-1})$ under $\mathbf{ex}_k$. Because $\mathbf{a}_{k-1}$ is reachable after the parser has processed W_{k-1} under the policy π_k, $P(S|\mathbf{a}_{k-1}, q_{k-1}, \mathbf{ex}_k) = P(S|W_k, \pi_k)$. In this way, we can map a tuple of the activation state and the control state $(\mathbf{a}, q)$ to a probability distribution over S under the constraint $\mathbf{ex}$. An important special case of this, with $k = 0$, allows us to estimate the unconditional distribution $P(S)$ by increasing q from 0 to q_{max} with $\mathbf{ex}_0 = \mathbf{0}$: this amounts to using the model as a *generator* as previewed in Section 1. This estimated distribution is $^*P(S)$.

3.3 Rational inference

Rational inference with w_k is defined as the update from $^*P(S|W_{k-1})$ to $^*P(S|W_k)$ given $^*P(S)$ where * indicates conditional probabilities computed by marginalizing $^*P(S)$ over cases where W_k were generated for the first k terminal roles.

The surprisal of w_k, $-\ln P(w_k|W_{k-1})$, equals the KL divergence between $^*P(S|W_{k-1})$ ($= P_{k-1}$) and $^*P(S|W_k)$ ($= P_k$) (Levy, 2008), which is the expected value of $(\ln P_k - \ln P_{k-1})$.

3.4 Optimal commitment policy

We define a commitment policy π to be optimal if, for every W_k, it minimizes the KL divergence $D_k = D(^*P(S|W_k)\|P(S|W_k, \pi_k))$. If the D_k are small, the parser approximates rational inference.

4 Surprisal as Harmony difference

The GSC parser processes a sentence word-by-word and processes every word in three phases. In this section, we argue that surprisal can be computed from the intermediate activation states directly and the value will be approximately proportional to the settling time in phase 1.

As the parser processes the k-th word in phase 1, the activation state changes from $\mathbf{a}_{k-1}^3$ to $\mathbf{a}_k^1$ under the influence of $\mathbf{ex}_k$. During this phase, q is fixed at q_{k-1}. When q and $\mathbf{ex}$ are fixed (all the other parameters are constant), the equilibrium probability density follows the Boltzmann distribution (Eq. 6) and the logarithm of the probability ratio of $P(\mathbf{a}_k^1)$ to $P(\mathbf{a}_{k-1}^3)$ can be computed as in Eq. 7.

$$P(\mathbf{a}) = \frac{e^{H(\mathbf{a})/T}}{\int e^{H(\mathbf{a}')/T} d\mathbf{a}'} \tag{6}$$

$$\ln P(\mathbf{a}_k^1) - \ln P(\mathbf{a}_{k-1}^3) = \frac{1}{T}(H(\mathbf{a}_k^1) - H(\mathbf{a}_{k-1}^3)) \tag{7}$$

where H is parameterized such that $q = q_{k-1}$ and $\mathbf{ex} = \mathbf{ex}_k$. Note that the LHS term of Eq. 7 corresponds to the KL divergence $D(P_k\|P_{k-1}) = E(\ln P_k - \ln P_{k-1})$ where $E(\cdot)$ is the expected value. Thus the surprisal at w_k is $E(\Delta H)/T$, with ΔH being the Harmony difference between the local optima before and after the input update.[7]

We can estimate the expected settling time t_c from the old to the new optimum by recalling that, on average, $d\mathbf{a}/dt = \nabla_\mathbf{a} H$, so:

$$\Delta H = \int_0^{t_c} \frac{dH(\mathbf{a})}{dt} dt = \int_0^{t_c} \nabla_\mathbf{a} H(\mathbf{a})^\top \frac{d\mathbf{a}}{dt} dt$$

$$\approx \int_0^{t_c} \|\nabla_\mathbf{a} H(\mathbf{a})\|^2 dt = t_c \cdot E(\|\nabla_\mathbf{a} H(\mathbf{a})\|^2)$$

where the approximation symbol indicates we ignore the stochastic term in Eq. 5. We approximate the average gradient with the average of the gradients at the initial and the final activation states $\mathbf{a}_{k-1}^3$ and $\mathbf{a}_k^1$. The gradient at $\mathbf{a}_k^1$ is $\mathbf{0}$ because $\mathbf{a}_k^1$ is the new optimum. The gradient at $\mathbf{a}_{k-1}^3$ can be calculated as follows: $\nabla_\mathbf{a} H(\mathbf{a}_{k-1}^3; q_{k-1}, \mathbf{ex}_k) = (\mathbf{ex}_k - \mathbf{ex}_{k-1}) + \nabla_\mathbf{a} H(\mathbf{a}_{k-1}^3; q_{k-1}, \mathbf{ex}_{k-1})$. Note that the last term is $\mathbf{0}$ because it was the optimum under $\mathbf{ex}_{k-1}$ (i.e., before the input word was updated) so the initial gradient is simply $(\mathbf{ex}_k - \mathbf{ex}_{k-1})$. It follows that the magnitude of the average of the initial and final harmony gradients in

---

[7] As the parser processes w_k, its state changes from $(\mathbf{a}_{k-1}^3, q_{k-1})$ through $(\mathbf{a}_k^1, q_{k-1})$ to $(\mathbf{a}_k^3, q_k)$, all of which have the same future under the influence of $\mathbf{ex}_k$. Thus, under an optimal commitment policy, $P_k = {}^*P(S|W_k) \approx P(S|\mathbf{a}_{k-1}^3, q_{k-1}, \mathbf{ex}_k) = P(S|\mathbf{a}_k^1, q_{k-1}, \mathbf{ex}_k)$. $P_{k-1} = {}^*P(S|W_{k-1}) \approx P(S|\mathbf{a}_{k-2}^3, q_{k-2}, \mathbf{ex}_{k-1}) = P(S|\mathbf{a}_{k-1}^3, q_{k-1}, \mathbf{ex}_{k-1})$.

phase 1 is constant for every w_k.[8] Thus, ΔH is approximately proportional to the settling time t_c.

In sum, surprisal of w_k, under an optimal commitment policy, is related to $\Delta H_k = H(\mathbf{a}_k^1; q_{k-1}, \mathbf{ex}_k) - H(\mathbf{a}_{k-1}^3; q_{k-1}, \mathbf{ex}_k)$ which in turn is proportional to settling time. In our model, surprisal has a geometrical meaning: it is the amount of hill climbing required to reach a new optimum due to the update of the word input.

5 Case study

We investigated a GSC model implementing a minimal probabilistic context-free grammar G = $\{p_1\ \text{S[1]} \rightarrow \text{A B}, p_2\ \text{S[2]} \rightarrow \text{A C}, p_3\ \text{S[3]} \rightarrow \text{D B}, p_4\ \text{S[4]} \rightarrow \text{D C}\}$ where p_k is the probability for the k-th sentence and $\sum_k p_k = 1$. Cho et al. (2017) used this minimal grammar (with $p_1 = p_2 = p_3 = p_4 = 0.25$) to investigate whether and how the GSC model can deal with computational challenges arising from local ambiguity. They argued that this language creates the core computational problems of incremental processing in the purest form. For example, after processing 'A' as a first word, an ideal incremental processing system must reject S[3](D,B) and S[4](D,C). At the same time, it must consider both S[1](A,B) and S[2](A,C) as candidate interpretations without choosing one over the other too early. They showed that the GSC model can achieve both computational goals by regulating commitment level q appropriately. When q increased too quickly or too slowly, the model respectively made "garden-path" errors (e.g., S[2](A,C) for an input sentence 'AB'; Bever, 1970; Frazier, 1987) or "local-coherence" errors (e.g., S[3](D,B) for an input sentence 'AB'; Tabor et al., 2004; Konieczny, 2005).

We investigated the same grammar G but we considered the cases where $p_1 \geq p_2$ because our interest is in the relationship between surprisal and processing times. To introduce a structural preference for S[1]/(A,B), a small value $\Delta h \in \{0, 0.1, 0.2, 0.3\}$ was added to the Grammar Harmony of S[1]-bindings (see Table 1 in Supplementary Material). (The model parameter Δh must be distinguished from ΔH discussed above). p_k was empirically estimated by running

---

the model as a generator (i.e., with no external input) 800 times.

5.1 Model

Figure 1 presents the GSC model implementing the grammar. Note that for a different choice of Δh, the parser implements a different PCFG. In addition to Δh, we manipulated T (see Eq. 5) in two levels (0.01 or 0.1) to see how the effect of Δh depends on T.

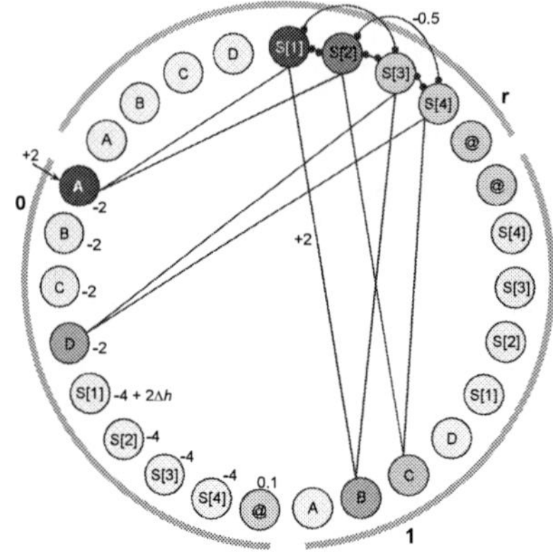

Figure 1: GSC implementation of grammar G via harmonic grammar rules. Only the implementation of grammatical constraints ($\mathbf{W}$ and $\mathbf{ex}$) are presented. The thick gray arcs show the grouping of bindings into different roles. Pairwise connections are bidirectional and implement binary HG rules. Every binding unit has a self-connection (implementing unary HG rules) and their values are presented near the binding units in role 0. The same fillers in other roles have the same negative self-connections as the filler in role 0. The arrow connecting to the binding A/0 indicates external input modeling the word input A as a first word. The colors of the binding units represent partial activation values (white=0, dark=1).

The GSC parser needs a commitment policy. Because every sentence of G is two words long, we considered a commitment policy $\pi = (q_0, q_1, q_2)$ where $q_0 = 0$, $q_2 = q_{max} = 15$, and q_1 was a free parameter.

5.2 Investigation of commitment policy

First, we investigated whether the GSC parser can approximate rational inference as introduced in Section 3. We considered 6 policies in which q_1 was set to one of the values (1, 3, 5, 7, 9, 11).

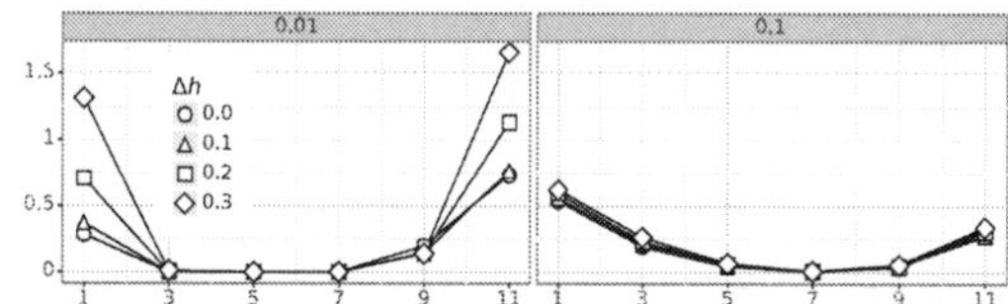 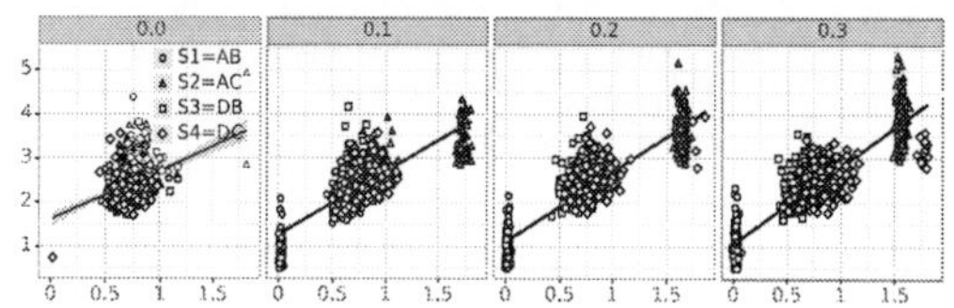

Figure 2: Plot of KL divergence of $^*P(S|W_2)$ from $P(S|W_2, \pi_2)$ against q_1 in $\pi_2 = (0, q_1, 15)$. Columns correspond to different T conditions.

Figure 3: Scatterplot of w_2 processing time (phase-1 duration) against ΔH. Different panels correspond to different Δh conditions. A linear fit line is overlaid in each panel.

Every model with a unique combination of Δh, T, and q_1 processed each of four sentences (S1=AB, S2=AC, S3=DB, S4=DC) word-by-word 200 times. By applying the algorithm introduced in Section 3, we estimated $P(S)$, $P(S|W_1, \pi_1)$, and $P(S|W_2, \pi_2)$. Because processing time was not of interest here, we excluded phase 1 and phase 3 as the parser processes each word. If dq/dt in phase 2 is small ($dq/dt = 1$ in the simulation), the omission of phase 1 and 3 does not change the result much. An optimal policy was defined as $(0, q_1, 15)$ that minimizes the divergence $D(^*P(S|W_k)\|P(S|W_k, \pi_k))$ averaged over W_k.

Because π_1 was fixed to $(q_0, q_1) = (0, 15)$, commitment policy does not play any role for the estimation of $P(S|W_1)$. The mean KL divergence from $P(S|W_1)$ to $^*P(S|W_1)$ across different first words were small (range=[0.001, 0.021] when $T = 0.01$ and [0.001, 0.020] when $T = 0.1$), suggesting the GSC parser approximates $^*P(S|W_1)$.

For w_2, we estimated $P(S|W_2, \pi_2)$ under each of the 6 policies. Figure 2 presents the average KL divergences of $^*P(S|W_2)$ from $P(S|W_2, \pi_2)$ as a function of Δh and T. When $T = 0.01$, the divergence was 0 when q_1 is either 5 or 7 in every Δh condition, suggesting the model parsed each of the four sentences accurately. When $T = 0.1$, the divergence was minimal (< 0.017) when $q_1 = 7$ for every Δh condition.[9]

5.3 Investigation of processing times

To investigate the relationship among harmony difference, surprisal (assuming rational inference), and word processing time, we chose the best of the commitment policies $\pi = (0, 5, 15)$ for the condition $T = 0.01$. Each of four GSC parsers, implementing different PCFGs (due to the different Δh values), processed each of four sentences 200 times under the best policy. Because the goal now

was to measure word processing time, all three phases were included in this simulation.

In Section 4, we argued that word processing time, more specifically, phase-1 settling time, must be must be proportional to HarmonyDifference $\Delta H_k = H(\mathbf{a}_k^1) - H(\mathbf{a}_{k-1}^3)$. Figure 3 presents w_2 phase-1 duration against ΔH_2, suggesting a linear trend.[10] In a regression analysis (Model 1A), we modeled w_2 phase-1 duration as a function of SentType (S1=AB, S2=AC, S3=DB, S4=DC to model processing of w_2 in context of w_1), NetID (a unique ID for each GSC parser with a unique Δh value), and HarmonyDifference. SentType and NetID were included to factor out manipulation-irrelevant variance so we do not report the estimates of their coefficients.[11] The coefficient of HarmonyDifference was significant: $b = 1.529$, $SE = 0.024$, $t = 64.919$, $p < .001$, supporting our claim. The adjusted R^2 statistic was 0.787 and $AIC = 3037$. We also tested whether $\ln(\Delta H)$ explains the phase-1 settling time well (Model 1B). The coefficient of log harmony difference was significant as well: $b = 0.445$, $SE = 0.008$, $t = 57.014$, $p < .001$. The adjusted R^2 stastistic was .755 and AIC was 3458, suggesting Model 1A explains processing time data slightly better.

In Section 3, we presented a method to derive a probability distribution over parses S from a tuple of an activation state and a control state q under ex and a commitment policy π. Based on this, we

---

[9] See Figures 1 and 2 in Supplementary Material for estimated probability distributions.

[10] The result was the same when total word processing time was used instead of phase-1 duration. This is because phase 2 has the same length for every sentence under the same policy and phase 3 settling time was not systematic in the current T setting. We present phase-1 duration data because it is theoretically related to harmony difference (Section 4).

[11] We did not include the interaction term between SentType and NetID because it covaried with harmony difference and surprisal. Recall that different levels of NetID are associated with different Δh values which in turn were used to create different surprisal values for different sentence types.

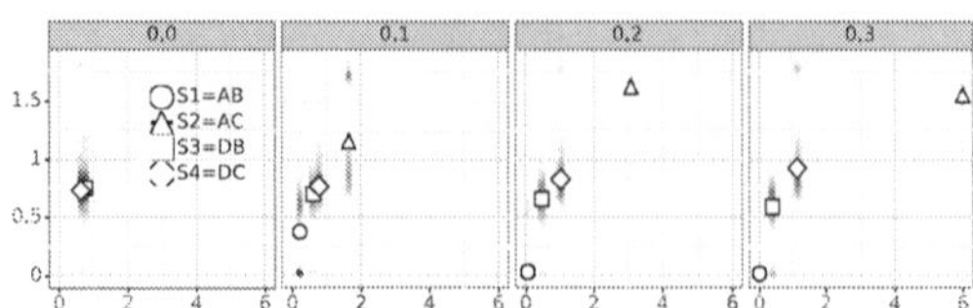

Figure 4: Scatterplot of ΔH_2 against surprisal of w_2 under rational inference. Different panels correspond to different Δh conditions.

argued that the harmony difference (scaled by T), can be interpreted as the parser-specific surprisal $D(P(S|W_k, \pi_k) \| P(S|W_{k-1}, \pi_{k-1}))$, which will be similar to surprisal under rational inference, $D(^*P(S|W_k) \| ^*P(S|W_{k-1}))$, under an optimal commitment policy. Thus, we predict harmony difference is a function of surprisal under rational inference under an optimal commitment policy.

Figure 4 presents harmony difference when the input word was updated from w_1 to w_2 against surprisal of w_2 under rational inference, suggesting a non-linear relationship between harmony difference and surprisal. In a regression analysis (Model 2A), we modeled harmony difference as a linear function of surprisal, controlling the effects of SentType and NetID. The coefficient of surprisal was significant: $b = 0.342$, $SE = 0.006$, $t = 53.933$, $p < .001$. The adjusted R^2 statistic was 0.786 and $AIC = -860.4$. In another regression analysis (Model 2B), we modeled harmony difference as a linear function of ln(surprisal). The coefficient of ln(surprisal) was significant: $b = 0.286$, $SE = 0.005$, $t = 60.984$, $p < .001$. The R^2 statistic was 0.811 and $AIC = -1259$, suggesting Model 2B better explains variance in ΔH.

We summarize the result in the following conceptual model: surprisal under rational inference $\rightarrow$ harmony difference (under an optimal commitment policy) $\rightarrow$ word processing time. In other words, harmony difference is the parser's actual surprisal under a commitment policy. The logarithm trend observed between surprisal and harmony difference needs further investigation but we consider two possibilities. First, the average magnitude of the actual gradient is systematically different depending on surprisal so our approximation introduces a bias. Second, although we chose the best commitment policy of 6 candidates, the chosen policy may not be optimal. Note that we used the same commitment policy for all four sentences. However, an optimal q_1 value may differ

for the first word A and the first word D.

6   General Discussion

An important research question concerning online sentence processing is to understand the source of processing difficulty. The surprisal hypothesis (Hale, 2001; Levy, 2008) provides a simple, intuitive, and general explanation at a computational level: processing difficulty is proportional to surprisal. The underlying mechanism is still beyond our understanding but researchers have started developing mechanistic accounts of surprisal (e.g., Rasmussen and Schuler, 2017). In this study, we tried to contribute to this line of research by providing a mechanism that relates surprisal to processing time via a stochastic, wellformedness-optimizing mechanism.

Our effort can be summarized as follows. First, the GSC model encodes structural uncertainty in the gradient activation of constituent symbols. An activation state at a given commitment level is analogous to the state of a symbolic parser but contains uncertainty information. It corresponds to a probability distribution over parses in the following sense: if the system starts from the given activation state and the given commitment level and is forced to choose a parse, it will choose different parses (grid points) with different frequencies (see Section 3).

Second, the model updates uncertainty in two ways: in response to the update of external information and via the control of commitment level. On the one hand, external input update makes the previously optimal activation state suboptimal so drives the system to a new optimum. In Section 4, we claimed that the amount of change required to travel from the old to the new optimum, harmony difference, can be interpreted as surprisal. There we showed why the settling time is proportional to the harmony difference. On the other hand, the internal control of commitment level is critical in holding the amount of structural ambiguity at an optimal level; this is implied in Figure 2 in Supplementary Material but was not the focus of this study. See Cho and Smolensky (2016) for the role of commitment policy.

Third, as we demonstrated in a simulation study (Section 5), the model can approximate rational inference under a good commitment policy and simulate the correlation between surprisal and processing time via harmony difference that is the parser's surprisal under the policy. There we reported the result that surprisal under rational inference explains variance in harmony difference, which in turn explains variance in processing time. In other words, surprisal under rational inference → harmony difference (the parser's surprisal) under a commitment policy → processing time.

An implication of our work is that surprisal is not a function of linguistic environment only, which we assume the parser learned well. From the GSC point of view, both the linguistic environment and the parser's commitment policy determine surprisal of each word input. For optimal sentence processing, the model needs both types of knowledge.

A limitation of our work is the simplicity of the grammar we investigated. We are actively investigating (with promising preliminary results) the model's ability to process more complex cases. But we point out that finding a good parameter setting and a good commitment policy, which can be challenging, is a separate issue from understanding the relation between surprisal and processing time. The present study focuses on the latter and the claim we made is generalizable.

Probabilistic models (e.g., Hale, 2001; Levy, 2008) provide a computational account of why and what problems must be solved in online language comprehension. Dynamical connectionist models (e.g., Tabor and Hutchins, 2004; Vosse and Kempen, 2009) provide a mechanistic account of why some sentences (e.g., garden-path sentences) take longer to process than others. By proposing how structural uncertainty can be encoded and updated in a symbolically-interpretable dynamical system model, our work bridges between these two general approaches to modeling human sentence processing.

Supplementary Material

Supplementary information is available at `https://goo.gl/uUudqx`.

Acknowledgments

We thank Geraldine Legendre, Akira Omaki, Kyle Rawlins, Ben Van Durme, and Colin Wilson for their contributions to this work, and gratefully acknowledge the support of NSF INSPIRE grant BCS-1344269. We thank Paul Tupper for suggesting the form of the H_C and H_Q functions used in this work.

References

Thomas G. Bever. 1970. The cognitive basis for linguistic structures. In John R. Hayes, editor, *Cognition and the Development of Language*, John Wiley, New York, pages 279–362.

Marisa Ferrara Boston, John Hale, Reinhold Kliegl, Umesh Patil, and Shravan Vasishth. 2008. Parsing costs as predictors of reading difficulty: An evaluation using the Potsdam Sentence Corpus. *Journal of Eye Movement Research* 2(1):1–12.

Pyeong Whan Cho, Matthew Goldrick, and Paul Smolensky. 2017. Incremental parsing in a continuous dynamical system: Sentence processing in Gradient Symbolic Computation. *Linguistics Vanguard* 3(1). https://doi.org/10.1515/lingvan-2016-0105.

Pyeong Whan Cho and Paul Smolensky. 2016. Bifurcation analysis of a Gradient Symbolic Computation model of incremental processing. In A. Papafragou, D. Grodner, D. Mirman, and J. C. Trueswell, editors, *Proceedings of the 38th Annual Conference of the Cognitive Science Society*. Cognitive Science Society, Austin, TX.

Vera Demberg and Frank Keller. 2008. Data from eye-tracking corpora as evidence for theories of syntactic processing complexity. *Cognition* 109(2):193–210. https://doi.org/10.1016/j.cognition.2008.07.008.

Lyn Frazier. 1987. Sentence processing: A tutorial review. In M. Coltheart, editor, *Attention and Performance XII: The Psychology of Reading*, Lawrence Erlbaum Associates, pages 559–586.

John Hale. 2001. A probabilistic Earley parser as a psycholinguistic model. In *Proceedings of the Second Meeting of the North American Chapter of the Association for Computational Linguistics on Language Technologies*. Association for Computational Linguistics, Stroudsburg, PA, USA, NAACL '01, pages 1–8. https://doi.org/10.3115/1073336.1073357.

John Hale. 2006. Uncertainty about the rest of the sentence. *Cognitive Science* 30(4):643–672.

John Hale and Paul Smolensky. 2006. Harmonic Grammars and harmonic parsers for formal languages. In Paul Smolensky and Géraldine Legendre, editors, *The Harmonic Mind: From Neural Computation to Optimality-Theoretic Grammar. Volume I: Cognitive Architecture*, The MIT Press, pages 393–416.

Daniel Jurafsky. 1996. A probabilistic model of lexical and syntactic access and disambiguation. *Cognitive Science* 20(2):137–194. https://doi.org/10.1016/S0364-0213(99)80005-6.

Lars Konieczny. 2005. The psychological reality of local coherences in sentence processing. In *Proceedings of the 27th Annual Conference of the Cognitive Science Society*. pages 1178–1183.

Roger Levy. 2008. Expectation-based syntactic comprehension. *Cognition* 106(3):1126–1177. https://doi.org/10.1016/j.cognition.2007.05.006.

Jill X. O'Reilly, Urs Schüffelgen, Steven F. Cuell, Timothy E. J. Behrens, Rogier B. Mars, and Matthew F. S. Rushworth. 2013. Dissociable effects of surprise and model update in parietal and anterior cingulate cortex. *Proceedings of the National Academy of Sciences* 110(38):E3660–E3669. https://doi.org/10.1073/pnas.1305373110.

Nathan E. Rasmussen and William Schuler. 2017. Left-Corner Parsing With Distributed Associative Memory Produces Surprisal and Locality Effects. *Cognitive Science* pages n/a–n/a. https://doi.org/10.1111/cogs.12511.

Nathaniel J. Smith and Roger Levy. 2013. The effect of word predictability on reading time is logarithmic. *Cognition* 128(3):302–319. https://doi.org/10.1016/j.cognition.2013.02.013.

Paul Smolensky. 1986. Neural and conceptual interpretation of PDP models. In *Parallel Distributed Processing: Explorations in the Microstructure of Cognition, Vol. 2: Psychological and Biological Models*, MIT Press, Cambridge, MA, pages 390–431.

Paul Smolensky. 1990. Tensor product variable binding and the representation of symbolic structures in connectionist systems. *Artificial Intelligence* 46(1):159–216. https://doi.org/10.1016/0004-3702(90)90007-M.

Paul Smolensky, Matthew Goldrick, and Donald Mathis. 2014. Optimization and quantization in gradient symbol systems: A framework for integrating the continuous and the discrete in cognition. *Cognitive Science* 38(6):1102–1138.

Paul Smolensky and Géraldine Legendre, editors. 2006. *The Harmonic Mind: From Neural Computation to Optimality-Theoretic Grammar. Volume 1: Cognitive Architecture*. The MIT Press, Cambridge, MA.

Whitney Tabor, Bruno Galantucci, and Daniel Richardson. 2004. Effects of merely local syntactic coherence on sentence processing. *Journal of Memory and Language* 50(4):355–370. https://doi.org/10.1016/j.jml.2004.01.001.

Whitney Tabor and Sean Hutchins. 2004. Evidence for self-organized sentence processing: Digging-in effects. *Journal of Experimental Psychology: Learning, Memory, and Cognition* 30(2):431–450. https://doi.org/10.1037/0278-7393.30.2.431.

Theo Vosse and Gerard Kempen. 2009. The Unification Space implemented as a localist neural net: Predictions and error-tolerance in a constraint-based parser. *Cognitive Neurodynamics* 3(4):331–346. https://doi.org/10.1007/s11571-009-9094-0.

Phonological (un)certainty weights lexical activation

Laura Gwilliams[1]   **David Poeppel[1]**   **Alec Marantz[1,2]**   **Tal Linzen[3]**

[1]Department of Psychology, New York University
[2]Department of Linguistics, New York University
[3]Department of Cognitive Science, Johns Hopkins University
{leg5, dp101, marantz}@nyu.edu   tal.linzen@jhu.edu

Abstract

Spoken word recognition involves at least two basic computations. First is matching acoustic input to phonological categories (e.g. /b/, /p/, /d/). Second is activating words consistent with those phonological categories. Here we test the hypothesis that the listener's probability distribution over lexical items is weighted by the outcome of both computations: uncertainty about phonological discretisation and the frequency of the selected word(s). To test this, we record neural responses in auditory cortex using magnetoencephalography, and model this activity as a function of the size and relative activation of lexical candidates. Our findings indicate that towards the beginning of a word, the processing system indeed weights lexical candidates by both phonological certainty and lexical frequency; however, later into the word, activation is weighted by frequency alone.

1 Introduction

There is mounting evidence for the predictive nature of language comprehension. Response times and neural activity are reduced in response to more predictable linguistic input. This indicates that the brain forms probabilistic hypotheses about current and future linguistic content, which manifest in expectations of phonemes, morphemes, words and syntactic structures (Connolly and Phillips, 1994; Lau et al., 2006; Lau et al., 2008; Ettinger et al., 2014; Gwilliams and Marantz, 2015).

In speech comprehension, the brain's task is to correctly determine a word's identity as quickly as possible. It is not optimal to always wait until word ending, because the target may be correctly identifiable earlier. For example, after hearing *hippopotamu-* the final /s/ provides very little additional information. Indeed, one could even stop at *hippot-* and still identify the target word correctly most of the time.[1]

How is this done? Upon hearing the beginning of a lexical item, the brain activates the cohort of words that are consistent with the acoustic signal. Words in the cohort are activated relative to their match to the phoneme sequence and frequency of occurrence. With each subsequent phoneme, the cohort is reduced as items cease to be consistent with the provided input, until one item prevails (see Figure 1). This process is consistent with the highly influential cohort model of spoken word recognition (Marslen-Wilson and Welsh, 1978; Marslen-Wilson, 1987), and has been associated with activity in left superior temporal gyrus (STG) (Gagnepain et al., 2012; Ettinger et al., 2014; Gwilliams and Marantz, 2015).

In practice though, phoneme identity is often uncertain: the acoustic signal may be consistent with both a [b] and a [p], for example. This phonetic uncertainty, and its effect on lexical activation, is not addressed by the cohort model. However, there is evidence suggesting that phonetic uncertainty affects lexical and sentential processing (Connine et al., 1991; McMurray et al., 2009; Bicknell et al., 2015).

Here we build upon this previous work in order to understand the neural computations underlying lexical activation, in service to spoken word recognition. Concretely, we ask: How does fine-grained acoustic information (below the phonological level) serve to activate lexical hypotheses and estimate their probabilities? Can this integration between phonological and lexical levels of description be read out from the STG?

---

[1]Note that *hippopotomonstrosesquippedaliophobia* ('fear of long words') and *hippopotas* ('a ground-type Pokemon') are also possible lexical items but much less frequent than the target in this case, so less likely to be selected.

Proceedings of the 8th Workshop on Cognitive Modeling and Computational Linguistics (CMCL 2018), pages 29–34,
Salt Lake City, Utah, USA, January 7, 2018. ©2018 Association for Computational Linguistics

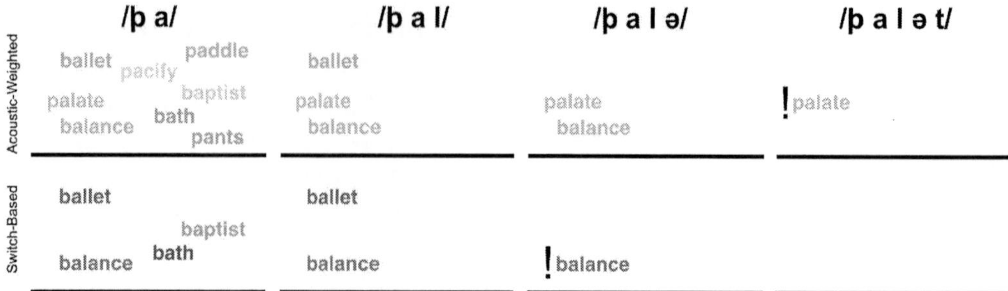

Figure 1: Schematic depiction of cohort activation under each of the two models, for the first five phonemes of the word *palate*. The onset b-p symbol represents that the onset phoneme was 75% consistent with a /b/ and 25% consistent with a /p/. Transparency reflects relative word activation. Note that the change in transparency between the two accounts reflects the actual probabilities predicted by each model — because there are more words activated in the Acoustic-Weighted account, less normalised probability is assigned to each item.

To address these questions, we model neural responses in STG, time-locked to each phoneme in a word, as a function of two computational models. One model assumes that the activation of a lexical candidate is gradiently weighted by the acoustic evidence in favour of that candidate: e.g., *balloon* is activated in proportion to how /b/-like the initial sound of the word was, even if that sound was more likely to represent a different phoneme (e.g., /p/). We refer to this model, in which phonetic uncertainty is carried over to the word recognition process, as the **acoustic-weighted** model. The other model assumes that acoustic information serves as a switch: a lexical item is either fully activated or not activated at all, as a result of a discrete decision made at the phonetic level. This model, which we refer to as the **switch-based** model, is most consistent with the traditional cohort model – the system commits to whichever phoneme is more likely, and this is used to form predictions at the lexical level (see Figure 1). A subset of the data reported here are also published in Gwilliams et al. (2017).

2 Summary of human data

2.1 Materials

Word pairs were selected such that, apart from the first phoneme, there was an identical phoneme sequence until a point of disambiguation. For example, *palate* and *balance* share their second, third and fourth phonemes ([æ], [l] and [ə], respectively), and diverge on the fifth ([t] vs. [n]). We selected 103 word pairs with this property. The onset of each word was either a voiced (d, b, g) or voiceless (t, p, k) plosive. A native English speaker was recorded saying each of these 206 words in isolation. The onset of each word was morphed along one phonetic feature, using the TANDEM-STRAIGHT software to create a 11-step continuum between word (e.g., *direct*) and non-word (e.g., *tirect*) (see Figure 2). The 11-step acoustic continuum was then re-sampled to form a 5-step perceptually defined continuum, based on the proportion of selections in a behavioural pre-test.

2.2 MEG experiment

Native English participants ($n = 25$) listened to each of the 103×5 words in isolation, and in 20% of trials (randomly distributed) made an auditory-to-visual word matching judgment.

While completing the task, neural responses were recorded using a 208-sensor KIT magnetoencephalography (MEG) system. Data were sam-

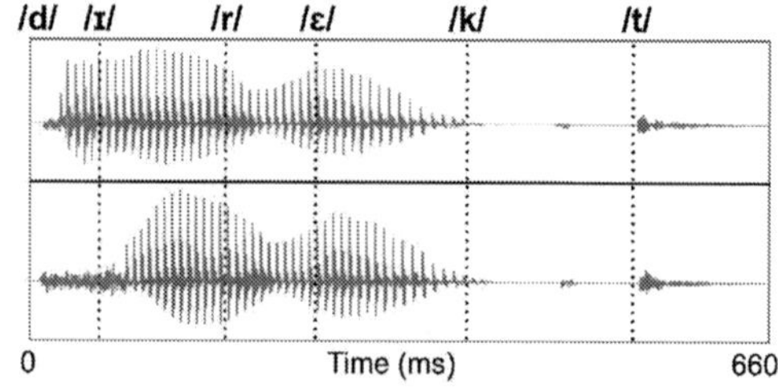

Figure 2: Waveforms of example endpoints of a lexical continuum. The word *direct* is above, and the non-word *tirect* is below. Dashed lines correspond to the timing of each phoneme onset.

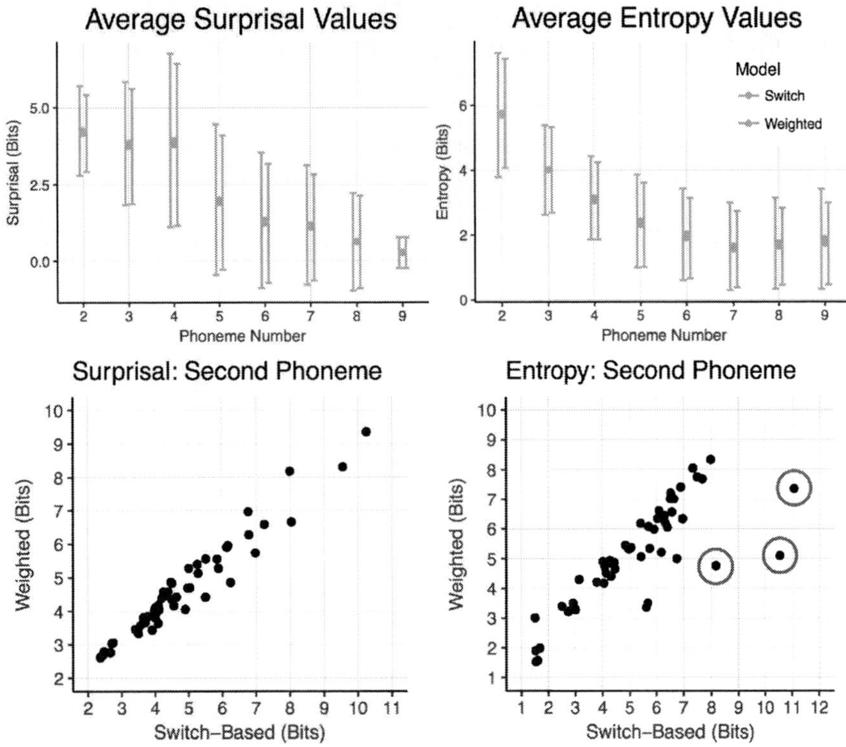

Figure 3: Top: Average surprisal and entropy values at each phoneme along the word. Note that not all words are 9 phonemes long, so phonemes at longer latencies contain fewer entries. Error bars represent one standard deviation from the mean. Bottom: Correlation between the two models' surprisal values and the two models' entropy values, at the second phoneme. Red circles highlight the outliers *topography*, *tirade* and *casino* (from right to left).

pled at 1000 Hz, which provided a measure of neural activity at each millisecond. In order to test responses to specific phonemes in a word, the data were cut into a series of 700 ms epochs, where the time at 0 ms corresponds to the onset of a phoneme. Note that the phonemes were shorter than 700 ms, so the epochs overlapped in time. The activity recorded from MEG sensors was localised using MNE-Python software (Gramfort et al., 2014), and averaged over the left STG. This provided one datapoint per millisecond (700) per phoneme (4370) per participant (25).

3 Modeling of MEG data

The variables of interest were entropy and surprisal. Entropy quantifies uncertainty about the resulting lexical item. For switch-based entropy we followed the typical calculation, which assumes that only the words whose phonemes are *most* consistent with the acoustics are included in the activated cohort (e.g., only the *b*-onset words):

$$-\sum_{w \in C} P(w|C) log_2 P(w|C) \qquad (1)$$

where C is the set of all words consistent with the heard prefix, and

$$P(w|C) = \frac{f(w)}{\sum_{w \in C} f(w)} \qquad (2)$$

where $f(w)$ is the frequency of the word w.

For acoustic-weighted entropy, the cohort is made up of two sub-cohorts, C_a and C_b, one for each of the possible word-initial phonemes (e.g., /b/ and /p/). The conditional probabilities of the words in each sub-cohort C_a and C_b were weighted by the probabilities of each possible onset phoneme given the acoustic signal A, which we derived from the behavioural pretest:

$$P(w|C, A) = \begin{aligned} &P(w|C_a)P(\varphi_a|A)+ \\ &P(w|C_b)P(\varphi_b|A) \end{aligned} \qquad (3)$$

where φ_a and φ_b are the two phonemes consistent with the acoustic signal A. These acoustic-weighted measures of word frequency and cohort frequency were then used in the typical entropy calculation given in Equation 1. We note that switch-based entropy can be understood as the result of rounding the acoustic weighting terms $P(\varphi_a|A)$ and $P(\varphi_b|A)$ to their nearest integer (either 1 or 0; see Figure 1).

Surprisal quantifies how expected the current phoneme φ_t is given the prior phonemes $\varphi_1, \ldots, \varphi_{t-1}$:

$$-log_2 \frac{f(\varphi_1, \ldots, \varphi_t)}{f(\varphi_1, \ldots, \varphi_{t-1})} \quad (4)$$

where $f(\varphi_1, \ldots, \varphi_t)$ denotes the summed frequency of all words that start with the phoneme sequence $\varphi_1, \ldots, \varphi_t$.

For switch-based surprisal, the conditional probability is calculated from the cohort of words most consistent with the acoustics at onset: e.g. the b-onset words. To calculate acoustic-weighted surprisal, we estimate the conditional probability separately for each cohort of words (a, b), and then scale each conditional probability by an acoustic weighting term and a lexical weighting term:

$$-log_2 \left(P(\varphi_a|A) \frac{f(\varphi_a, \varphi_2, \ldots, \varphi_t)}{f(\varphi_a, \varphi_2, \ldots, \varphi_{t-1})} Q_a^t + P(\varphi_b|A) \frac{f(\varphi_b, \varphi_2, \ldots, \varphi_t)}{f(\varphi_b, \varphi_2, \ldots, \varphi_{t-1})} Q_b^t \right) \quad (5)$$

where

$$Q_a^t = \frac{f(\varphi_a, \varphi_2, \ldots, \varphi_t)}{f(\varphi_a, \varphi_2, \ldots, \varphi_t) + f(\varphi_b, \varphi_2, \ldots, \varphi_t)} \quad (6)$$

The Q lexical weighting is the probability of the observed sequence, given a cohort that contains both φ_a and φ_b-onset words. The acoustic weighting is the same as described above.

In all, this surprisal value is calculated by estimating the probability of each phoneme φ_a, φ_b given i) acoustics; ii) preceding phonemes; iii) probability of the sequence given a joint cohort. The probability of each phoneme is then summed before taking the negative logarithm. This derives an overall surprisal of the sound, given the phonological categories it could realise.

For all of these calculations, word frequencies were extracted from the English Lexicon Project (Balota et al., 2007).

As shown in Figure 3, the surprisal and entropy calculations from the two models were highly correlated. This is because here we are re-analysing a dataset that was designed and collected for other reasons. In future work we plan to design materials that maximally distinguish switch-based and acoustic-based accounts. Our results stand in as a first approximation that can (and should) be built upon.

4 Results

The dependent measure was activation of left STG, averaged between 200-250 ms after phoneme onset, a time window determined based on Ettinger et al. (2014). This activity was modelled time-locked to each phoneme along the length the word, but we primarily focused on the second (mean post-onset latency = 87 ms; SD = 25 ms, 4021 observations) and the sixth phonemes (mean post-onset latency = 411 ms; SD = 78 ms, 3264 observations). This was because they included a similar number of trials in each model comparison, while also ensuring substantial differences in latency from word onset. Reported results were corrected for multiple comparisons over all six phoneme positions using Bonferroni correction. Only responses to partially ambiguous trials were included (0.25 and 0.75), because this is where the predictions of acoustic-weighted and switch-based models are most distinct.

We evaluated the fit of the predictions of each model to the neural measurement using a linear mixed effects model. The full model contained switch-based and acoustic-weighted surprisal, switch-based and acoustic-weighted entropy, phoneme latency, trial number, block number, stimulus amplitude of the first 30 ms, phoneme pair and ambiguity as fixed effects. By-subject slopes were included for all entropy and surprisal predictors. This full model was compared to a model where either acoustic-entropy and surprisal, or switch-based entropy and surprisal, were removed as fixed effects (but remained as by-subject slopes). This gave a statistical assessment of the amount of variance the acoustic-weighted and switch-based models were accounting for.

At the second phoneme, the acoustic-weighted variables explained a significant amount of variance ($\chi^2 = 5.02$, $p = .025$), whereas the switch-based variables did not ($\chi^2 = 2.62$, $p = .1$).

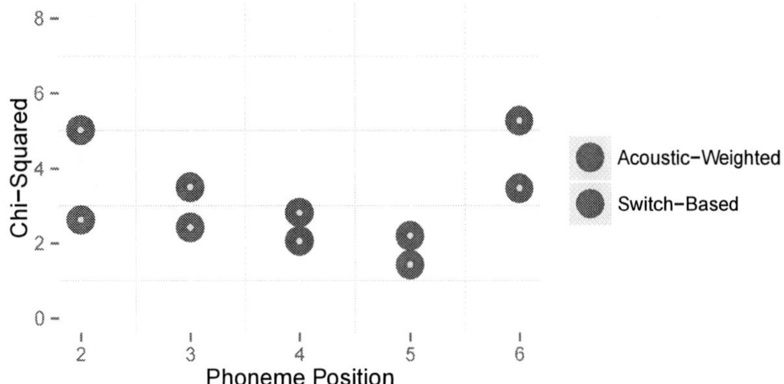

Figure 4: Reduction in linear mixed-effects model log-likelihood resulting from excluding acoustic-weighted surprisal and entropy (in red) or switch-based surprisal and entropy (in blue); higher values indicate that the predictors increase model fit more. The dependent measure was activity averaged from 200-250 ms in STG, time-locked to phonemes along the length of the words.

At the third phoneme, the acoustic-weighted variables were marginally significant ($\chi^2 = 3.49$, $p = .061$), the switch-based variables were not ($\chi^2 = 2.41$, $p = .12$). At the fourth phoneme, neither model was significant: Acoustic weighted ($\chi^2 = 2.05$, $p = .15$) or switch-based ($\chi^2 = 2.81$, $p = .094$). The same was true at the fifth phoneme: Acoustic weighted ($\chi^2 = 2.19$, $p = .14$), switch-based ($\chi^2 = 1.42$, $p = .23$). At the sixth phoneme, we observe the opposite effect from the second phoneme position: the switch-based variables explained a significant amount of variance ($\chi^2 = 5.26$, $p = .022$) and the acoustic-weighted variables had only marginal explanatory power ($\chi^2 = 3.46$, $p = .06$). These results are displayed in Figure 4.

5 Discussion

We have found evidence that the brain uses fine-grained acoustic information to weight lexical predictions in spoken word recognition. At the beginning of a word, lexical hypotheses are activated in proportion to the bottom-up acoustic evidence; towards the end, acoustic evidence acts as a switch-like function, to either fully activate or deactivate the word, bounded by its frequency of occurrence. This finding has two primary implications.

First, it suggests that the system does not wait until phonological categories have been disambiguated before activating lexical items. Rather, uncertainty about phonological classification is used to modulate higher level processes, ensuring that phonological discretisation is not a bottleneck in activating lexical items. This supports interactive models of speech processing, because it suggests that the output of one stage does not need to be determined before initiating the following. In particular, this finding is inconsistent with the Cohort model of speech perception (Marslen-Wilson and Welsh, 1978), which assumes that the system first commits to the most likely phoneme before making lexical predictions.

Second, it suggests that the same processing strategy is not heuristically applied in all situations. Rather, phonological information appears to be used more when processing the beginning of a word than the end. There are two explanations for this. This could reflect that the system commits to a particular phonological category after a given delay period, and so the phonological weights used by the system converge to a stable decision point. Or perhaps lexical frequency becomes more informative as the size of the cohort decreases, and so phonological detail is given less predictive power by the processing system. A simple way to tease these alternatives apart in future work is to manipulate the ambiguity of phonemes within a word, not just in initial position. The former would predict that acoustic evidence is used in close proximity to the ambiguous sound, regardless of its position in the word; the latter would predict that acoustic evidence is used more at the beginning of the word, regardless of the position of the ambiguous sound.

References

David A. Balota, Melvin J. Yap, Keith A. Hutchison, Michael J. Cortese, Brett Kessler, Bjorn Loftis, James H. Neely, Douglas L. Nelson, Greg B. Simpson, and Rebecca Treiman. 2007. The english lexicon project. *Behavior Research Methods*, 39(3):445–459.

Klinton Bicknell, Michael K. Tanenhaus, and Florian Jaeger. 2015. Listeners can maintain and rationally update uncertainty about prior words. *Manuscript submitted for publication.[KB]*.

Cynthia M. Connine, Dawn G. Blasko, and Michael Hall. 1991. Effects of subsequent sentence context in auditory word recognition: Temporal and linguistic constraints. *Journal of Memory and Language*, 30(2):234–250.

John F. Connolly and Natalie A. Phillips. 1994. Event-related potential components reflect phonological and semantic processing of the terminal word of spoken sentences. *Journal of Cognitive Neuroscience*, 6(3):256–266.

Allyson Ettinger, Tal Linzen, and Alec Marantz. 2014. The role of morphology in phoneme prediction: Evidence from meg. *Brain and Language*, 129:14–23.

Pierre Gagnepain, Richard N. Henson, and Matthew H.Davis. 2012. Temporal predictive codes for spoken words in auditory cortex. *Current Biology*, 22(7):615–621.

Alexandre Gramfort, Martin Luessi, Eric Larson, Denis A. Engemann, Daniel Strohmeier, Christian Brodbeck, Lauri Parkkonen, and Matti S. Hämäläinen. 2014. MNE software for processing MEG and EEG data. *Neuroimage*, 86:446–460.

Laura Gwilliams and Alec Marantz. 2015. Non-linear processing of a linear speech stream: The influence of morphological structure on the recognition of spoken arabic words. *Brain and language*, 147:1–13.

Laura Gwilliams, Tal Linzen, David Poeppel, and Alec Marantz. 2017. In spoken word recognition the future predicts the past. *bioRxiv*, page 150151.

Ellen Lau, Clare Stroud, Silke Plesch, and Colin Phillips. 2006. The role of structural prediction in rapid syntactic analysis. *Brain and Language*, 98(1):74–88.

Ellen Lau, Colin Phillips, and David Poeppel. 2008. A cortical network for semantics:(de) constructing the N400. *Nature Reviews Neuroscience*, 9(12):920–933.

William D. Marslen-Wilson and Alan Welsh. 1978. Processing interactions and lexical access during word recognition in continuous speech. *Cognitive Psychology*, 10(1):29–63.

William D. Marslen-Wilson. 1987. Functional parallelism in spoken word-recognition. *Cognition*, 25(1-2):71–102.

Bob McMurray, Michael K. Tanenhaus, and Richard N. Aslin. 2009. Within-category vot affects recovery from lexical garden-paths: Evidence against phoneme-level inhibition. *Journal of Memory and Language*, 60(1):65–91.

Predicting and Explaining Human Semantic Search in a Cognitive Model

Filip Miscevic
Cognitive Science Program,
Complex Networks & Systems
Indiana University Bloomington
fmiscevi@iu.edu

Aida Nematzadeh
Department of Psychology
University of California
Berkeley
nematzadeh@berkeley.edu

Suzanne Stevenson
Department of Computer Science
University of Toronto
suzanne@cs.toronto.edu

Abstract

Recent work has attempted to characterize the structure of semantic memory and the search algorithms which, together, best approximate human patterns of search revealed in a semantic fluency task. There are a number of models that seek to capture semantic search processes over networks, but they vary in the cognitive plausibility of their implementation. Existing work has also neglected to consider the constraints that the incremental process of language acquisition must place on the structure of semantic memory. Here we present a model that incrementally updates a semantic network, with limited computational steps, and replicates many patterns found in human semantic fluency using a simple random walk. We also perform thorough analyses showing that a combination of both structural and semantic features are correlated with human performance patterns.

1 Human Semantic Processing

The study of human semantic memory—word meanings, their relations, and their storage—is challenging due to the complexity of factors involved. Finding (1) the right representation for word meanings and their relations, (2) the mechanism responsible for learning the representation, (3) the appropriate search algorithm to efficiently retrieve information from semantic memory, and (4) the suitable empirical data to evaluate the proposed representations and algorithms is a difficult task. Previous research has extensively explored each of these (*e.g.*, Collins and Loftus, 1975; Steyvers and Tenenbaum, 2005; Griffiths et al., 2007).

Psychologists frequently use a task known as semantic fluency (or verbal fluency) to examine human semantic representation and processing (Troyer et al., 1997; Ardila et al., 2006). Participants are asked to produce as many words as they can from a given category (*e.g.*, animal) in a fixed amount of time (*e.g.*, three minutes). The resulting data—which words people recall and in what order—can shed light on how people represent word meanings and their relationships, and how they search such semantic information. For example, Hills et al. (2012) found that participants tend to reply in semantically-related bursts of words— *e.g.*, they recall words from the pet subcategory of animals (*dog, cat*) then switch to a different subcategory, such as African animals (*lion, zebra*), etc.—indicating that people tend to follow a strategy of *exploiting* a semantically-related patch of words, then *exploring* to find a new patch, much like animals foraging in their environment.

Recent work has investigated the properties of semantic representations and processing algorithms that can account for this type of behavior in the semantic fluency task. Different researchers have found that a match to human behavior can be achieved in either of two ways: (a) using a simple (vector-based) semantic representation in combination with an informed, two-stage algorithm to exploit and explore the space (Hills et al., 2012); or (b) creating a richer representation—structured as a semantic network—and using a simple random walk to access it (Abbott et al., 2015; Nematzadeh et al., 2016). These findings suggest that the choice of representation and search algorithm are interdependent, such that the same empirical data can be replicated through different combinations of representation and algorithm that make different trade-offs on the locus of complexity (Abbott et al., 2015).

However, if both combinations account for the

Proceedings of the 8th Workshop on Cognitive Modeling and Computational Linguistics (CMCL 2018), pages 35–45,
Salt Lake City, Utah, USA, January 7, 2018. ©2018 Association for Computational Linguistics

human data considered thus far, the question of which model more plausibly captures what occurs in a search in human semantic memory remains open. As Abbott et al. (2015) suggest, further experiments, such as those performed by Hills et al. (2015), can help elucidate the differences between these approaches to modelling human semantic memory. In particular, if there are key aspects of human semantic search that can be explained by one model and not the other, then this goes towards disconfirming the latter. One of the goals of the current paper is to show that a random walk over a semantic network reproduces even the additional empirical patterns of human semantic fluency task examined by Hills et al. (2015).

In addition to these experimental approaches, other findings and theoretical considerations may come to bear on resolving the question of which model most aptly reflects human semantic search.

For example, people appear to have a structured semantic memory that encodes many kinds of relational knowledge (Miller and Fellbaum, 1991). In this way, complexity costs are incurred during learning (while creating the structured representation) rather than every time the representations are accessed. As such, accessing the knowledge later becomes a more efficient process. Hence, it may be reasonable to suggest that a simple search algorithm operating over a structured semantic network is a preferable model.

Another open issue is precisely what kind of semantic representations realistically capture word relations, especially semantic similarity, which typically form the basic structure of a semantic network (*e.g.*, Miller and Fellbaum, 1991). Work modeling human semantic fluency behavior using a simple random walk over a semantic network has drawn on several different kinds of semantic word representations. Abbott et al. (2015) constructed their semantic network using human association norms (Nelson et al., 1998), so that weighted edges between words directly capture the similarities between them that are relevant to the fluency task (Jones et al., 2015). Nematzadeh et al. (2016) built two networks based on different semantic representations learned from text corpora: a simple vector-based representation model, called BEAGLE, learned from Wikipedia (Jones and Mewhort, 2007, previously used by Hills et al. (2012)), and probability distributions learned from child-directed corpora (Fazly et al., 2010).

Given that a random walk over semantic networks from each of these sources—human association norms, vector-space representations, and probability distributions—all model human fluency behavior, how do we choose between them?

An important set of considerations that we explore here involves the cognitive plausibility of how a semantic representation could be learned. While the human association norms used by Abbott et al. (2015) accurately reflect human judgments of word relatedness, it is unclear how the similarity assessments captured in such norms can be learned through language exposure.

The BEAGLE vector-space representations, on the other hand, are learned from instances of natural language. However, acquisition is a batch process over Wikipedia data, which is arguably not a good proxy for the linguistic input from which individuals acquire their semantic lexicon. The probability distributions used by Fazly et al. (2010), however, are learned by a cognitive model from a corpus of child-directed speech. These representations thus meet important criteria for cognitive plausibility, in that they are learned from naturalistic linguistic input.

One final crucial issue that has remained unaddressed to date is the incremental learnability of the semantic network structure itself. Children simultaneously learn word meanings as well as the relations between them (Jones et al., 1991). Thus, it is important to model the simultaneous incremental learning of both semantic word representations and their structure in a semantic network. This has been neglected by previous work discussed so far. Even in the work where semantic representations are learned, only the word representations and not their relations are learned. Instead, the semantic network is created by exhaustively comparing all the word representations after training—a process that is too computationally demanding to be cognitively plausible.

Our contributions in this paper are threefold: First, we show that a semantic network created incrementally within an online word learning model—from naturalistic child language acquisition data—can yield human performance in semantic search using a simple random walk. Our work here confirms that a semantic network created and updated incrementally—while the model is learning words—has the appropriate structure to yield patterns observed in the semantic fluency task, despite having noisy and incomplete connections as a result of being generated from partial knowledge acquired at each time step. Second, as mentioned, we show that the new approach to creating the semantic network produces a structure that also mimics other aspects of human behavior in semantic fluency, going beyond earlier models in the scope of empirical data accounted for (Abbott et al., 2015; Nematzadeh et al., 2016).

Finally, we extend previous analyses of semantic organization to determine more precisely which network properties are correlated with the observed human performance patterns. While other work has focused on the importance of structural properties of the network in determining human behavior (Goñi et al., 2010; Steyvers and Tenenbaum, 2005), we find that both structural *and* semantic properties are necessary to generate patterns observed in human semantic fluency data.

2 Incremental Network Creation

We use the approach of Nematzadeh et al. (2014) to incrementally build a semantic network, which draws on the probabilistic cross-situational word learning model developed by Fazly et al. (2010).

2.1 Incremental Word Learning Model

The semantic network is generated from word meanings (representations) learned by the model of Fazly et al. (2010), trained on the Manchester corpus (Theakston et al., 2001) of the CHILDES database (MacWhinney, 2000). Each input to the model consists of an *utterance* from the corpus, labelled with a *scene* consisting of semantic features for each word. For example, consider the following utterance (U) and selected features from its accompanying scene (S):

U: {*look, at, the, monkey, eat, a, banana*}
S: { ..., VERTEBRATE, MAMMAL, ..., FRUIT, ... }

Just as a child must learn the referent of each word in a sentence, the learner must infer which features in the scene are associated—or *aligned*—with each word. The model captures this association as the probability of a feature f given a word w, $P(f|w)$, which it incrementally updates from the co-occurrence of f with w across all observed utterance–scene pairs. The meaning of each word w is then represented as the probability distribution $P(\cdot|w)$ over all semantic features, which is estimated through latent variables that model the possible alignments of words and features in an

utterance–scene pair. An incremental Expectation Maximization algorithm is used to update $P(\cdot|w)$ (Neal and Hinton, 1998). Hence, as in children, word meanings are gradually learned after many exposures to utterances and scenes.

In particular, for a single utterance–scene pair processed at time t, the alignment (a) probability of each feature (f_i) in the scene and word in the utterance (w_j) is calculated by:

$$P_t(a_{ij}|f_i) = \frac{P_{t-1}(f_i|w_j)}{\sum_{w' \in u} P_{t-1}(f_i|w')}$$

$P_{t=0}(f_i|w_j)$ is initially randomly uniformly distributed. Once the alignment probabilities are calculated, the word meanings are updated:

$$P_t(f_i|w_j) = \frac{\sum_{u \in U_t} P_t(a_{ij}|u, f_i)}{\sum_{f' \in M_t} \sum_{u \in U_t} P_t(a_{ij}|u, f')}$$

Here, U_t represents the set of utterances processed up to and including time t, and M_t is the set of features observed up to and including time t. Note that the summations do not have to be calculated anew each time; the terms from the first $t-1$ utterances can be stored and updated with the contributions from the tth utterance–scene pair.

The learned representation for a word, $P(\cdot|w)$, can be treated as a vector representation of the word over all semantic features. In the present study, we focus on animal nouns, as they are the target of the semantic fluency task in humans. The semantic features of noun meanings used are derived from WordNet hypernyms (Fellbaum, 1998, `http://wordnet.princeton.edu`), and embed hierarchical conceptual knowledge of nouns.

The more features (hypernyms, in this case) two animal words (*e.g.*, "CAT","DOG" vs. "CAT","FROG") have in common, the more similar their learned representations. The model learns not only the features associated with that particular word, however, but also features that often occur in the same context as the word. For example, in the above utterance–scene pair, the model may come to associate a non-zero probability with the feature FRUIT and the word *monkey*. Hence, the learned meanings of words capture not only a conceptual hierarchy for that word but also information learned from the context of their usage.

2.2 Incremental Learning of Semantic Networks

Children do not just learn the meanings of words, they also learn the relations between them at the same time (Jones et al., 1991). We use the approach taken by Nematzadeh et al. (2014) to enable the model to learn word meanings and the relationships between them simultaneously, without exhaustively considering all possible relationships between the words.

Since the probability distribution $P(\cdot|w)$ for a given word w is stored as a vector over all semantic features, the cosine of the angle between them can be computed as a measure of their similarity. A semantic network can thus be constructed by representing each word as a node in the network, with an edge between them if the cosine similarity between two words is greater than a threshold ρ.

Whenever a new utterance–scene pair U–S is processed, the probabilities $P(\cdot|w_u)$ of all $w_u \in U$ are updated, affecting the cosine similarities between words w_u and all other words. The semantic network must be updated to reflect these changes in cosine similarities—*i.e.*, some edges may be added, some removed, some changed in weight. However, rather than calculating the (new) cosine similarities between each w_u and *all* other words, the model use a limited set of calculations. It first updates the current edges connecting w_u to its neighbors. Then it selects a small set of new words w_i that *potentially* have a high probability of being similar to w_u. This is accomplished by incrementally forming semantic clusters over word meanings that are adjusted when a word's meaning is updated (Anderson and Matessa, 1992). Each newly updated word meaning w_u is compared to an average (*i.e.*, prototype) representation of each cluster to determine its probability of belonging to that cluster. Finally, n words are selected from each cluster and their cosine similarity to w_u updated, where n is proportional to the probability of w_u belonging to that cluster. The number of computations is limited as w_u is only compared to the cluster prototypes and a restricted number of words from each cluster.

By limiting the number of computations at each step of learning, the model is more cognitively plausible than exhaustively updating the semantic network after each utterance. However, it also means that the resulting semantic network will be noisy—it may have missing, superfluous or incorrectly-weighted edges.

3 Experimental Data and Approach

In this section, we explain the details of the semantic fluency experiment as well as the seman-

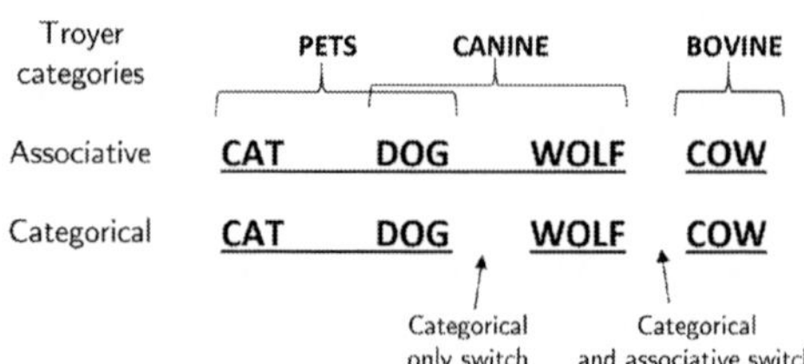

Figure 1: The difference between categorical and associative patch switches, based on Hills et al. (2015).

tic representation and search algorithm used in our simulations. All of the code and data necessary to reproduce our experiments are available at `https://github.com/FilipMiscevic/random_walk`.

3.1 Evaluation: Semantic Fluency Data

We evaluate our simulations using data from a semantic fluency experiment in which participants were tasked with naming as many animals as they can in three minutes (Hills et al., 2012, 2015). Hills et al. (2012) inferred that the recalled words (*e.g.*, *dog*, *cat*, *lion*, *zebra*) form semantically-related categories or "patches", based on their inter-item retrieval times (IRT)—the time elapsed between the naming of two sequential items that have not previously been recalled. They find that the IRT increases as search within a semantically-related category progresses. A switch into a different semantic category occurs when the IRT exceeds the participant's average IRT across the entire trial. The IRT then decreases and the pattern begins again (see Figure 2a). This result shows that participants exhibit different behavior when recalling words from within a semantic category compared to switching into a new semantic category. Hills et al. (2012) argue that this pattern is a consequence of an informed two-stage search process: local cues, such as similarity to the most recent response, are used to search within patches, and global cues, such as the overall frequency of a word, are used to switch into new patches. Here we replicate previous results that demonstrate that the IRT pattern (Figure 2a) can be predicted by a simple search given structured representations (Abbott et al., 2015; Nematzadeh et al., 2016). In addition, we show that this process matches other patterns observed in the semantic fluency experiment (Hills et al., 2015).

3.2 Representation: A Semantic Network

We assume words and their relations are structured as a semantic network—a graph whose nodes are words, and edges reflect the similarity between the word meanings. We compare two sets of semantic networks, one set created *after training* the word learner explained in Section 2.1, while the other is built *incrementally during the training*, as described in Section 2.2. While the model learns many words, we only consider animal words, as we can evaluate those against the semantic fluency experiment of Hills et al. (2012). We also include the word *animal* itself in the semantic networks, as this is the cue word used in the experiment.

Two words w_i and w_j are connected in the semantic network if the cosine similarity between their feature vectors, $P(\cdot|w_i)$ and $P(\cdot|w_j)$, is above the threshold, $\rho = 0.8$. An exception is made for words connected to the word *animal*: because *animal* is a hypernym of the other animals, its cosine similarity will be less than the cosine between animals of the same subcategory. As such, to ensure that *animal* remains connected to some words in the network, edges radiating from it are kept if the similarity is at least $\rho_{animal} = 0.4$. Both models learn the representations of all 93 animal words present in the corpus; however, not all nodes are guaranteed to be connected to the rest of the network due to this thresholding. These thresholds were determined by a grid search over the possible values of ρ and ρ_{animal} (*i.e.*, $(0, 1]$). The model predicts the human data over a notable range of parameter values; nonetheless, there are still more networks in that parameter space that do not predict the data. In Section 5, we will explore what characteristics of the networks are responsible for their successful prediction of data.

Batch Network. The word learner was trained on 120k utterance–scene pairs, with the meaning representation of a word, $P(\cdot|w)$, calculated as described in Section 2.1. After training has concluded, a semantic network is constructed using the final learned representations. A total of 70 words is present in this network.

Incremental Network. The learner is trained on 28k utterance–scene pairs.[1] After each utterance–scene pair is processed, the connections in the semantic network are updated as described in Section 2.2. A total of 75 words is present in this network.

Note that although the word representations of each model are learned by the same learning algorithm, they produce very different semantic net-

works. In the Batch Network, the edges are created only after training is completed, and is accomplished by exhaustively computing the cosine similarity between all word-pair combinations. The Incremental Network, on the other hand, uses a more cognitively plausible approximation of this process whereby edges are incrementally created by comparing only a small percentage of the word pairs.[2] This means that relations captured by the edges of the Incremental Network are noisier and incomplete.

The Incremental Network still only approximates the process of semantic acquisition in people, albeit more plausibly compared with previous work. As described above, however, we empirically set two thresholds that determine whether words are connected or not: one for the word *animal* and another one for all other animal words. Future work will need to explore whether this distinction can be learned while the network is incrementally created.

3.3 Search Algorithm: A Random Walk

We model the search process as a random walk in which semantic information is retrieved by randomly visiting nodes in the semantic network. Recall that in the semantic fluency experiment, the participants were cued by the word *animal* and were asked to name as many animals they can in three minutes. Following Abbott et al. (2015), we simulate this experiment by performing a weighted random walk on each network, beginning with the word *animal*. At each step in the random walk, a neighboring node is visited with a probability proportional to the edge weight connecting them, and the visited word is stored. Just as repeated words are not considered in the human recall data, we assume the output of a random walk to be the sequence of unique words encountered—*i.e.*, each word is counted in the output only when retrieved for the first time. The number of steps taken before the walk terminates (including steps to already-visited nodes) is 70, which produces about the same number of words on the networks as human participants on average do (*i.e.*, 37 ± 5). The results we report are averages over 300 such walks.

---

[1]Even with the smaller corpus (28k as opposed to 120k input pairs), the model predicts the semantic fluency data; thus, we used the smaller corpus to speed up our simulations.

[2]This ends up being only 8% of all $\frac{n(n-1)}{2}$ possible comparisons at each time step, where n is the total number of words seen by the learner at each time step.

3.4 Analyzing Random Walks

In the semantic fluency task, the human response patterns are reflected in changes in the inter-item retrieval time (IRT) over the list of responses. In the empirical data, IRT is the time elapsed from one word until the next word is recalled, and increases and decreases are observed as people switch from one semantic patch of words to another, as noted above. Thus, to evaluate the random walks in our semantic networks against this IRT pattern, we must define a measure of time in the simulated walks (since actual model speed is not an appropriate proxy). We also must determine what constitutes a patch and a switch between two patches.

3.4.1 Measuring Time and Semantic Distance

We follow Abbott et al. (2015) in defining the IRT in a random walk on a semantic network as the number of steps taken (i.e., number of edges crossed) between two words. More specifically, we define IRTs for our walks as follows: for each word that has not previously been visited by the random walk, the IRT is the number of steps taken in the random walk since the last word that was seen for the first time. For example, if the model visits the sequence of nodes "CAT,DOG,CAT,RAT", the random walk output is "CAT,DOG,RAT", and the IRT between CAT and DOG is 1, whereas the IRT between DOG and RAT is 2.

The IRT is considered a proxy for semantic distance between the words. Hills et al. (2015) also looked directly at semantic distances in the sequences generated in the human fluency task: They used vector-space representations (of the BEAGLE model) to calculate cosine similarity between consecutive words. As such, in addition to using IRT in assessing our walks, we also draw on the cosine similarities between words.

3.4.2 Identifying Patch Switches

Each word in a random walk is labeled by the category/categories it belongs to, as defined by Troyer et al. (1997). Words (*e.g.*, DOG) can belong to more than one category (*e.g.*, PETS, CANINE). As a result, there are different possibilities for defining what constitutes a patch and where the patch switches occur. We explore two different ways of defining patches over Troyer's categories, following Hills et al. (2015), as summarized in Figure 1.
Categorical patch switch. A patch switch occurs when a word in the sequence has no category in

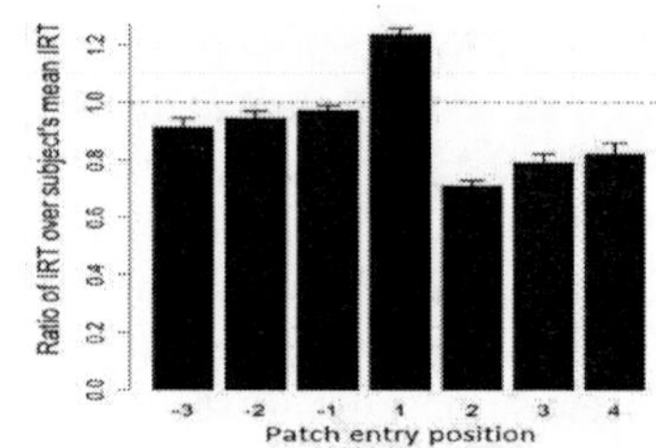

(a) Human data

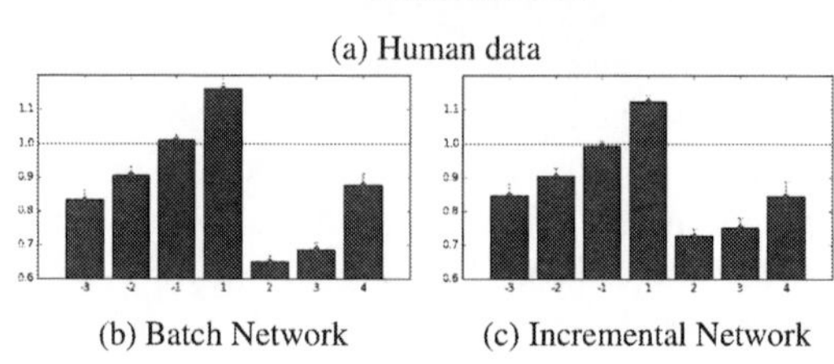

(b) Batch Network   (c) Incremental Network

Figure 2: (a) Human IRTs reproduced from Hills et al. (2012). (b,c) IRTs from random walks generated from the simulated semantic networks. Bars are SEM.

common with *all* of the words in the current patch. In the sequence "CAT,DOG,WOLF", "DOG,WOLF" is a patch switch because WOLF is not in the same category as CAT (is not a PET).
Associative patch switch. A patch switch occurs when a word in the sequence has no category in common with the *last* word in the patch. For example, "DOG,WOLF" is not a patch switch because both words share the Troyer category CANINE, but "WOLF,COW" is a patch switch because they have no categories in common.

From this definition it follows that all associative patch switches are also categorical patch switches. However, a categorical patch switch may not be associative; one such "categorical only" patch switch is illustrated in Figure 1. Hills et al. (2015) argue that human search through memory is more like an associative search, and that the associative patch switch model better explains human IRT patterns. We use the associative patch switch model except where explicitly comparing the differences between the alternatives.

4 Predicting Semantic Fluency Data

Here we compare the results of random walks over the Batch and Incremental Networks in mimicking human semantic fluency data. First, we focus on predicting the pattern of recall observed in human data, then we examine the properties of each patch switch model.

4.1 Recall Patterns

In the human semantic fluency data (Figure 2a), the longest IRTs tend to occur between successive words that do not share a semantic category, presumably reflecting their greater distance in semantic memory (Hills et al., 2012, 2015). This is referred to as a patch switch. In the figure, a patch entry position of 1 indicates the average IRT between the first item in a patch and the item retrieved before it. Similarly, a patch entry position of -1 is the average IRT between the two items preceding a patch switch. Human IRTs in patch entry position 1 (patch switch) are higher than the average IRT, as people take longer to switch to a new patch, then dip below the average IRT at patch position 2 as people recall words within a patch.

As Hills et al. (2012) point out, this behavior is consistent with the marginal value theorem (MVT) of optimal foraging for patches of food in physical space (Charnov, 1976). In particular, MVT demonstrates that to maximize foraging gains, the optimal moment to leave a current patch is when the instantaneous reward drops below the average reward. In the human semantic search task, since participants are asked to retrieve as many words as they can, shorter IRTs lead to a bigger 'reward', as more words can thus be retrieved within the time limit. Indeed, Hills et al. (2012) demonstrated that those subjects whose search patterns conformed with MVT retrieved the most words. We evaluate whether the IRT patterns of our models also conform to the predictions of MVT as observed in the human data. As such, the first patch-entry position IRT must be significantly greater than the mean IRT (e.g., the ratio between the two is greater than 1) and all other patch entry positions must be no greater than the mean IRT. Finally, successive IRTs within the same patch should be non-decreasing.

As shown in Figure 2, we observe a similar pattern to the human IRT data in both the Batch and Incremental Networks: the IRT drops between the first and second items in a patch, then steadily increases until the IRT exceeds the long-term average IRT, reflecting a patch switch. A single-sided t-test confirms that the first patch entry IRT is greater than the average IRT ($p \ll 0.001$). We accept the null hypothesis that the patch entry IRT at position -1 is no greater than the average IRT ($0.08 \le p \le 0.20$). The other IRTs are significantly less than the average IRT ($p < 0.02$) and successive IRTs within a patch are indeed non-decreasing. This demonstrates, for the first time, that the combination of a simple search

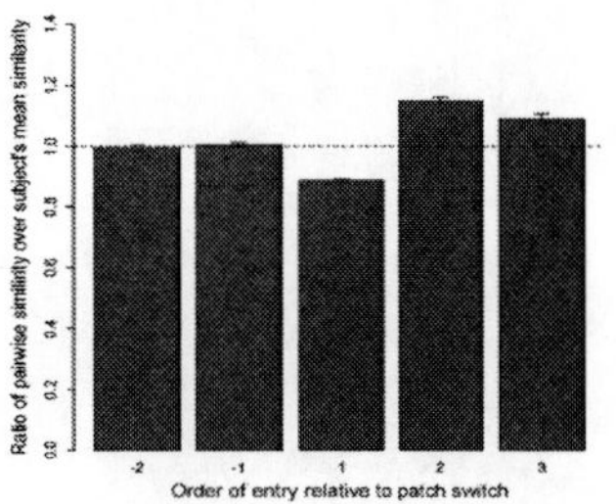

(a) Human data

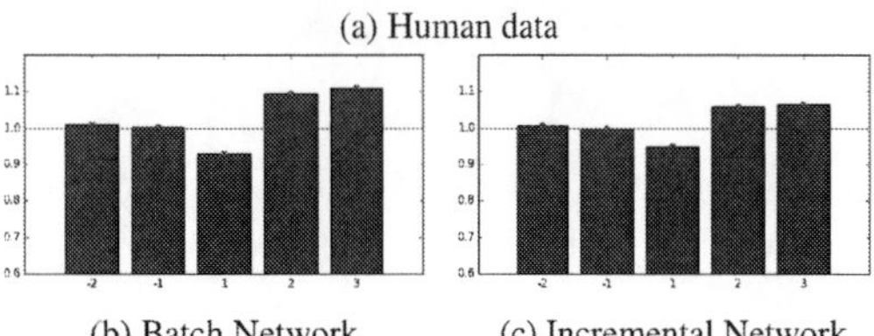

(b) Batch Network   (c) Incremental Network

Figure 3: Cosine similarities between words in successive patch positions normalized by the average long-term cosine similarity in (a) BEAGLE vectors for items retrieved by humans (Hills et al., 2012), (b,c) our semantic networks.

and structured representation that is incrementally created—simultaneously, as words are learned—can predict basic patterns observed in human semantic fluency. Next, we model additional aspects of the human data that have not been considered in previous work (Abbott et al., 2015; Nematzadeh et al., 2016).

A roughly analogous pattern with respect to patch entry positions is found with the average cosine similarities, although here, because cosine represents similarity rather than distance, the direction is reversed, as seen in Figure 3. Words at a patch switch are the least similar to one another. Again, the first patch entry position cosine similarity is significantly less than the average cosine simimlarity ($p < 0.05$). The other patch entry position cosines are on average no smaller than the average ($p \ge 0.05$). This supports the notion that words within patches are more similar (and hence, closer in semantic memory) to each other than words between patches.

4.2 Patch Switch Type Proportion and Duration

Hills et al. (2015) categorize patch switches on the human data by whether they are associative or categorical-only (see Figure 1). Two observations are made from this data. Firstly, as in Figure 4a, the proportion of associative patch switches steadily increases throughout the four quartiles of the walk, but the number of categorical-only patch switches stays the same.

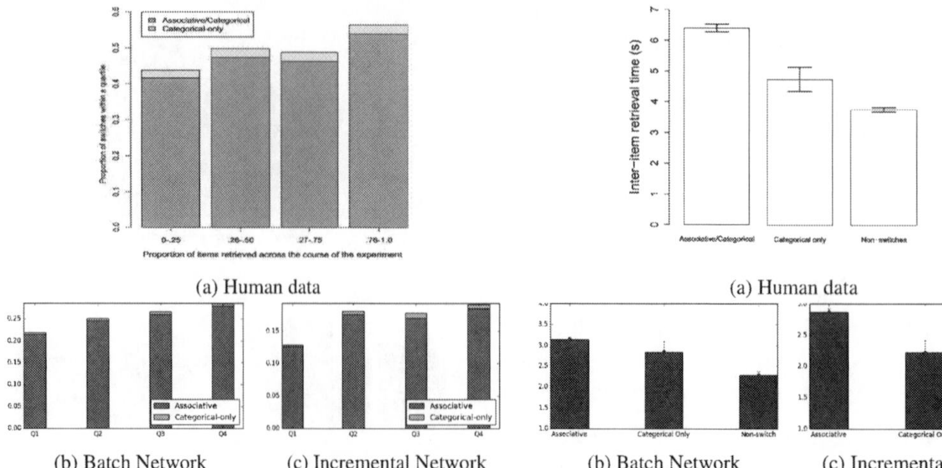

(a) Human data

(b) Batch Network   (c) Incremental Network

Figure 4: Average proportion of patch switch type on each quartile of the random walk for (a) human data (Hills et al., 2012), (b,c) our semantic networks.

(a) Human data

(b) Batch Network   (c) Incremental Network

Figure 5: Average IRTs based on patch switch types for (a) human data (Hills et al., 2012), (b,c) our semantic networks.

This suggests that as more words are retrieved and semantic patches are depleted, new semantic patches must be explored. However, the categorical-only switches do not change in frequency. We speculate this may either be because they do not contribute to the need to explore different patches, or that they are so uncommon to begin with.

Secondly, as in Figure 5a, associative and categorical-only switches take longer than non-switches, which is expected, as non-switches search within a patch of semantically-related words. Associative switches take the longest, as they delineate the boundaries between the most semantically-different categories (compared to categorical-only switches).

Model Predictions. When we subject the random walks on our networks to these analyses, we observe the same pattern (Figures 4,5). This is the first work to confirm that a random walk on semantic network is consistent with the observed pattern on the duration and proportion of different types of switches.

Hills et al. (2015) point out the associative patch switch model has a *Markov property*, insofar as that only the proceeding word's category affects the existence of a patch switch with the next word. This is an interesting observation because it suggests that the associative switches may simply be easier to make, as only the previous word's categories affect the transition to the current word. In contrast, a categorical-only switch demands higher memory overhead as the next word is af-

fected by the overall category/categories shared by members in the current patch. Our results show that a random walk on a structured semantic network can predict the timing and proportion of these different types of switches.

5 Explaining Semantic Fluency Data

While our results confirm that a simple search on an incrementally-created semantic network mimics many aspects of semantic fluency behavior, not all the semantic networks predict aspects of the human data, such as adherence to MVT. Adding edges to the semantic network depends on the similarity between words reaching a certain threshold. We experimented with a wide range of thresholds on similarity of word pairs (see Section 3.2) and observed that patterns consistent with MVT, as in the human IRT data (Figure 2a), appear only within a certain parameter range. Since the choice of threshold affects the overall structure of the semantic network, we explore the features that distinguish those semantic networks that reproduce human semantic fluency patterns from those that do not.

Previous research has emphasized that semantic networks representing human knowledge have particular structural properties; namely, a small-world structure, as explained below (Steyvers and Tenenbaum, 2005). However, Nematzadeh et al. (2016) observe that having a small-world structure is not a sufficient condition to guarantee a match to observed human behavior in semantic search. A factor that has remained unexplored is how the quality of a network's semantic connections—

whether semantically similar words are connected through a path—affects a network's ability to replicate findings in human semantic search. We hypothesize that this semantic quality is also important in predicting semantic fluency data, because even two networks identical except for node labels would produce very different behavior as the relationships between the words they represent would be completely different.

Here we perform an extensive analysis considering both structural and semantic properties of the networks to assess which features contribute to the model's adherence to MVT, a major pattern in the human data. By identifying these features, we can better understand the salient aspects of semantic memory that give rise to patterns in human semantic search. We first explain how we measure the structural and semantic features of the networks. Then we discuss how we build a regression model to determine which features are responsible in predicting the semantic fluency data.

5.1 Measuring Structure and Semantics

A network exhibits small-world structure if it is sparse and highly connected at the same time— there are not a lot of edges in the network, but most nodes are connected through a set of high-degree nodes. As a result, the network consists of a set of highly-connected components that are connected through the high-degree nodes. Small-worldness is often quantified by σ:

$$\gamma = \frac{C}{C_{random}}, \qquad \lambda = \frac{L}{L_{random}}, \qquad \sigma = \frac{\gamma}{\lambda}$$

where C is the average local clustering coefficient and L is the average path length, and the subscript *random* refers to the metric of an equivalent Erdős-Renyi network. A network is considered to be small-world when $\sigma > 1$ (or more strictly, $\gamma \gg 1$, $\lambda \approx 1$) (Watts and Strogatz, 1998). Intuitively, $\gamma \gg 1$ reflects a structure of tightly connected components in the network, and $\lambda \approx 1$ reflects relatively short path distances between nodes compared to a random network.

We observe that all of the semantic networks capable of reproducing the human patterns are small-world, but not all small-world networks generate these patterns, which is consistent with the findings of Nematzadeh et al. (2016). As a result, we consider other structural and semantic features. The structural features include the number of vertices ($|V|$), number of edges ($|E|$), and the sparsity

of the network (average nodal degree).

Quality of semantic connections. In addition to the structure of a network, we examine the quality of its semantic connections. We explore this by first identifying the semantic clusters formed in each network using the HDBSCAN algorithm (Campello et al., 2013), and then evaluating these clusters using Troyer's categories as our gold-standard data Troyer et al. (1997). We assume that each cluster in the network can have exactly one category (e.g., pets). To determine the category label of a cluster, we examine the Troyer category memberships of each of its words, and assign the category label based on which category is shared by the most words of the cluster.

We use the standard measures of precision, recall, and F-score to assess the quality of each cluster, and average these across all clusters, weighted by cluster size, to obtain weighted precision, weighted recall, and weighted F-score for a network. We also consider the number of clusters in each network as a feature, $|H|$.

5.2 Analyzing the Contribution of Features

We characterize which structural and semantic features of a network are most important (in predicting human data) by fitting logistic regression models on all possible combinations of features.

Prior to training, feature values were transformed into z-scores (i.e., for a given feature x for a given network i, the standardized value is $(x_i - \bar{x})/\hat{s}$; $\bar{x}$ is the sample mean of the feature for all networks and $\hat{s}$ is sample standard deviation). This permits the coefficients of regression to be compared directly in terms of their contribution in predicting the data.[3]

5.2.1 Experimental Set-Up

Logistic classifier models were trained on a set of Batch and Incremental networks. During training, we ensure an equal representation of networks that adhere to and do not adhere to MVT. This is a binary condition satisfied according to the criteria explained in Section 4.1. Networks were first generated across the entire parameter space of the similarity thresholds (i.e., all combinations of ρ and ρ_{animal} ranging from 0 to 1, in increments of

---

[3] Although some of these features are dependent (*e.g.*, $|E|$ and *sparsity*), we do not include their interactions in our regression analysis. We focus on understanding whether a subset of individual features can explain the human data and thus examine all possible combinations of features.

0.1). We excluded networks where the number of nodes reachable by the starting word 'animal' was smaller than 30, as they would not be able to produce as many words as human participants did (37 ± 5) (Hills et al., 2012). Since the number of non-IRT producing networks outnumbered the IRT producing networks, we uniformly sampled the parameter space in which IRT pattern-producing networks occurred so that the number of each would be equal. Using this procedure, 42 Batch and 56 Incremental networks were generated. In each case, exactly half of the networks produce the IRT pattern consistent with MVT.

Model selection. For each set of Batch and Incremental networks, we examine which features best predict the human data by building and evaluating logistic regression models for all combinations of features. Model selection was performed in two steps. First, the models with the highest stratified-3-fold (SKF) cross-validation score were taken. From these, the model with the fewest number of features was selected.

5.2.2 Results of Logistic Regression

Table 1 shows the features that appeared in the logistic regression model that achieved the best SKF cross-validation score for each of the types of networks. Since each feature was standardized (with $mean = 0$ and $variance = 1$), the magnitude of the coefficients can be interpreted directly. We note that small-worldness (σ) and weighted F-score are influential predictors for both Batch and Incremental networks. In both models, weighted F-score is the most influential predictor. Although σ is the least influential predictor, we find it significant that it is a shared predictor for both networks. Structural properties relating to the number of edges ($|E|, sparsity$) as well as clustering coefficient (C, γ), are structural properties that have been previously characterized in semantic networks (Steyvers and Tenenbaum, 2005; Goñi et al., 2010). Hence, we conclude that both topological features—namely, small worldness (high clustering coefficient and short average path length)—and semantic features—high weighted F-score (good precision and recall in clusters)—are jointly associated with reproducing the IRT pattern.

6 Conclusions

Learning word meanings and representing them in semantic memory are processes that often oc-

Networks	Acc.	Features and Coefficients				
Batch	93%	**σ**	λ	C	sparsity	**weighted F-score**
		0.58	0.74	-1.92	0.94	**0.94**
Incremental	90%	**σ**	γ	$|E|$		**weighted F-score**
		0.65	0.71	-1.64		**1.07**

Table 1: Features used to train the logistic regression models for predicting IRT pattern production with the highest stratified 3-fold cross-validation accuracy (Acc.). Shared features are bolded.

cur simultaneously, notably in early language acquisition. A cognitive model capable of integrating these two processes will therefore more realistically capture language acquisition and usage. It is noteworthy that both the Batch and Incremental Networks perform comparably on all of the data examined here. We consider this strong support for the hypothesis that semantic networks learned incrementally on a naturalistic language corpus can replicate search patterns in the free recall task, a claim that is neither obvious nor trivial to demonstrate. Furthermore, some of the performance characteristics we use in measuring the fit of the model to the human data—namely, whether the IRT patterns produced by the model are consistent with MVT or not—are binary conditions: either the behavior is replicated or it is not, so, barring additional criteria, a graded scale by which to score performance is not possible. Future work will seek to better characterize the performance differences between the two models.

We deploy a model that can generate semantic networks incrementally from naturalistic language use, *i.e.* child-directed speech, while it gradually learns the word meanings, lending it plausibility as a cognitive model. We show this model replicates human performance on semantic fluency tasks; namely, with regards to patch entry IRT, patch entry cosine similarity patterns, patch switch type proportions, and patch switch type IRTs. We show, furthermore, that the Markov property of the random walk does indeed align with the associative nature of search in the human semantic fluency task (Hills et al., 2015).

By investigating the structural and semantic features of these and other networks, we show that small-worldness alone does not explain the ability of a network to replicate the human patterns. Having highly connected components, *and* ones that reflect the semantic categories of words, are both properties that may be necessary in predicting semantic search behavior observed in humans.

References

Joshua T Abbott, Joseph L Austerweil, and Thomas L Griffiths. 2015. Random walks on semantic networks can resemble optimal foraging. *Psyc. Rev.* 122(3).

John R. Anderson and Michael Matessa. 1992. Explorations of an incremental Bayesian algorithm for categorization. *Machine Learning* 9(4):275–308.

Alfredo Ardila, Feggy Ostrosky-Sols, and Byron Bernal. 2006. Cognitive testing toward the future: The example of semantic verbal fluency (animals). *International Journal of Psychology* 41(5):324–332. https://doi.org/10.1080/00207590500345542.

Ricardo J. G. B. Campello, Davoud Moulavi, and Joerg Sander. 2013. Density-based clustering based on hierarchical density estimates. *PAKKD 2013* .

Eric L Charnov. 1976. Optimal foraging, the marginal value theorem. *Theoretical Population Biology* 9(2):129–136.

Allan M. Collins and Elizabeth F. Loftus. 1975. A spreading-activation theory of semantic processing. *Psyc. Rev.* 82(6):407.

Afsaneh Fazly, Afra Alishahi, and Suzanne Stevenson. 2010. A probabilistic computational model of cross-situational word learning. *Cog. Sci.* 34(6):1017–1063.

Christiane Fellbaum, editor. 1998. *WordNet, An Electronic Lexical Database*. MIT Press.

Joaquín Goñi, Gonzalo Arrondo, Jorge Sepulcre, Iñigo Martincorena, Nieves Vélez de Mendizábal, Bernat Corominas-Murtra, Bartolomé Bejarano, Sergio Ardanza-Trevijano, Herminia Peraita, Dennis P. Wall, and Pablo Villoslada. 2010. The semantic organization of the animal category: evidence from semantic verbal fluency and network theory. *Cognitive Processing* 12:183–196.

Thomas L. Griffiths, Mark Steyvers, and Joshua B. Tenenbaum. 2007. Topics in semantic representation. *Psyc. Rev.* 114(2):211.

Thomas T Hills, Michael N Jones, and Peter M Todd. 2012. Optimal foraging in semantic memory. *Psyc. Rev.* 119(2):431.

Thomas T Hills, Peter M Todd, and Michael N Jones. 2015. Foraging in semantic fields: How we search through memory. *Topics in Cognitive Science* 7:513–534.

Michael N Jones, Thomas T Hills, and Peter M Todd. 2015. Hidden processes in structural representations: A reply to Abbott, Austerweil, and Griffiths (2015). *Psyc. Rev.* 122(3).

Michael N Jones and Douglas JK Mewhort. 2007. Representing word meaning and order information in a composite holographic lexicon. *Psyc. Rev.* 114(1):1.

Susan S. Jones, Linda B. Smith, and Barbara Landau. 1991. Object properties and knowledge in early lexical learning. *Child Development* 62(3):499–516.

Brian MacWhinney. 2000. *The CHILDES Project: Tools for Analyzing Talk*, volume 2: The Database. Erlbaum, 3rd edition.

G. A. Miller and C. Fellbaum. 1991. Semantic networks of English. *Cognition* 41(1–3):197–229.

Radford M. Neal and Geoffrey E. Hinton. 1998. A view of the EM algorithm that justifies incremental, sparse, and other variants. In *Learning in graphical models*, Springer, pages 355–368.

Douglas L Nelson, Cathy L McEvoy, and Thomas A Schreiber. 1998. The University of South Florida free association, rhyme, and word fragment norms .

Aida Nematzadeh, Afsaneh Fazly, and Suzanne Stevenson. 2014. A cognitive model of semantic network learning. In *Proceed. Conf. on Empirical Methods in Natural Lang. Processing*.

Aida Nematzadeh, Filip Miscevic, and Suzanne Stevenson. 2016. Simple search algorithms on semantic networks learned from language use. In *Proceedings of the 38th Annual Conference of the Cognitive Science Society*.

Mark Steyvers and Joshua B. Tenenbaum. 2005. The large-scale structure of semantic networks: Statistical analyses and a model of semantic growth. *Cog. Sci.* 29(1):41–78.

Anna L. Theakston, Elena V. Lieven, Julian M. Pine, and Caroline F. Rowland. 2001. The role of performance limitations in the acquisition of verb–argument structure: An alternative account. *Journal of Child Language* 28:127–152.

Angela K. Troyer, Morris Moscovitch, and Gordon Winocur. 1997. Clustering and switching as two components of verbal fluency: Evidence from younger and older healthy adults. *Neuropsychology* 11(1):138–146.

Duncan J. Watts and Steven H. Strogatz. 1998. Collective dynamics of 'small-world' networks. *Nature* 393(6684):440–442.

Modeling bilingual word associations as connected monolingual networks

Yevgen Matusevych, Amir Ardalan Kalantari Dehaghi and **Suzanne Stevenson**
Department of Computer Science, University of Toronto
`yevgen@cs.toronto.edu`
`amirardalan.kalantaridehaghi@mail.utoronto.ca`
`suzanne@cs.toronto.edu`

Abstract

Word associations are a common tool in research on the mental lexicon. Studies report that bilinguals produce different word associations in their non-native language than monolinguals, and propose at least three mechanisms responsible for this difference: bilinguals may rely on their native associations (through translation), on collocational patterns, and on the phonological similarity between words. In this paper, we first test the differences between monolingual and bilingual responses, showing that these differences are consistent and significant. Second, we present a computational model of bilingual word associations, implemented as a semantic network paired with a retrieval mechanism. Our model predicts bilingual word associations better than monolingual baselines, and translation is the main mechanism explaining its success, while collocational and phonological associations do not improve the model.

1 Introduction

In a free association task, participants are given a cue word (e.g., *apple*) and produce the first word that comes to their mind (e.g., *red* or *fruit*).[1] Free associations have been a common tool in the study of the mental lexicon because the observed pattern of associations can reflect the nature and strength of connections between words in semantic memory.

We focus on free associations as a means to better understand the structure and processing of the mental lexicon in bilinguals. Bilingual word associations have been studied for decades (see an

overview in Meara, 2009). Despite a number of important findings, which we summarize in the following section, high-level conclusions about the association norms in bilinguals' non-native language are unclear – not only because of high variability in bilingual populations (DeKeyser, 2013), but also due to methodological factors (as explained by Boulton, 2003; Krzemińska-Adamek, 2014). Of specific concern for us is the lack of robust statistical analyses of the results. Many studies provide a selective qualitative analysis of the responses, and their findings can be inconsistent. In particular, it is unclear whether there are significant differences between native and non-native word associations (as compared, for example, to the instability of responses within a group of speakers over time).

We address this issue by providing a statistical analysis of the differences in English word association responses of Dutch[L1]–English[L2] bilinguals (collected by van Hell and de Groot, 1998) compared to English monolingual word association norms. After demonstrating a quantifiable difference between them, we then present the first computational model of bilingual word associations, which we use to investigate how the structure and processing of the bilingual lexicon could lead to the observed differences.

2 Related work

2.1 Non-native word associations

In general, non-native speakers' responses tend to differ from those of native speakers (e.g., Wolter, 2001; Zareva, 2007; Antón-Méndez and Gollan, 2010; Hui, 2011). Non-native speakers often produce responses that are translation equivalents of responses they would give in their native language (Meara, 1978) – in other words, L1 *mediates* their L2 responses (Nam, 2014). Such translations are produced more frequently when the cue word and

---

[1] In a so-called continued version of this task, participants give more than one response, but for consistency we always consider only the first response to each cue in this study.

Proceedings of the 8th Workshop on Cognitive Modeling and Computational Linguistics (CMCL 2018), pages 46–56,
Salt Lake City, Utah, USA, January 7, 2018. ©2018 Association for Computational Linguistics

its translation are cognates[2] (Taylor, 1976; van Hell and de Groot, 1998). Also, collocational responses (called 'syntagmatic'; e.g., *duty–free, opportunity–take*: Politzer, 1978; Riegel and Zivian, 1972) and phonological responses (*favor–flavor*: Meara, 1978; Namei, 2004) tend to be produced by non-native speakers more frequently than by monolinguals. Multiple examples of all these effects are well-documented, yet open questions remain regarding how systematic these differences are between bilinguals and monolinguals.

Van Hell and de Groot (1998, henceforth vHdG) carry out a free association experiment with Dutch–English bilinguals (i.e., native Dutch speakers who have been learning English). For us, their study is interesting in two respects. First, vHdG work with two similar groups of bilinguals and test one of the groups twice, which allows us to measure the consistency of responses between two groups of bilinguals, as well as within a single group. Second, large-scale monolingual association norms are available for both Dutch and English, which helps us both with our statistical analyses and in building a computational model. We use vHdG's data (1) to carry out a systematic comparison of monolingual and bilingual responses, and (2) to train and test a computational model that helps us predict whether the effects described above are systematic or not.

2.2 Existing computational models

Graph-based models (or semantic networks) have been widely used in research on semantic memory (see an overview by Beckage and Colunga, 2016). Despite their 'localist' approach in which a word is simply represented by a node (rather than using distributed representations), such models are a useful tool in the study of lexical access and acquisition. In particular, they have successfully replicated patterns of human verbal behavior in free word association (Enguix et al., 2014; Gruenenfelder et al., 2015), semantic fluency tasks (Abbott et al., 2015; Nematzadeh et al., 2016), lexical growth/acquisition (Stella et al., 2017; Bilson et al., 2015), assessment of semantic similarity (Jackson and Bolger, 2014; De Deyne et al., 2016), etc.

Naturally, a graph is only a static representation of the lexicon, although its structure presumably reflects lexical processing (Beckage and Colunga, 2016). To simulate the actual processing dynam-

ics, various mechanisms have been proposed, such as spreading activation, random walk, entanglement, etc. (Galea et al., 2011; Zemla and Austerweil, 2017). In a spreading activation model, the activation starts at a given node and spreads across the graph over adjacent edges proportionally to edge weights (Anderson, 1983; Roelofs, 1992). Recently, De Deyne et al. (2016) used this approach on a free association graph to predict human similarity judgments for weakly-related concepts. We use a similar approach to model bilingual free associations in our computational model.

3 Data analysis

While vHdG explored various aspects of bilingual word associations, they did not compare the bilingual responses they collected to independent monolingual data. Here, we quantitatively compare vHdG's data against monolingual association norms, to see whether the non-native responses are indeed systematically different from those of native speakers. As vHdG argue, there is a lot of variability among bilinguals. Therefore, we need to compare the between-group differences (monolinguals vs. bilinguals) against within-group differences (two sets of bilinguals), to ensure that any between-group difference we find is due to more than the variation in responses among bilinguals.

3.1 Distance measures

Our goal is to compare two sets of responses to a particular cue word against each other. For this, we use two measures. The first is based on average precision, widely used in information retrieval. This measure treats one (unordered) set of responses as a gold standard and compares this set against another (ordered) set, considering only the top n responses. Because we are interested in measuring the *distance* between the two sets, we employ a complementary measure ρ to assess the distance between an unordered (shorter) set X and an ordered (longer) set Y:

$$\rho_n(X, Y) = 1 - \frac{\sum_{k=1}^{n} \left(P_k(X, Y) \times 1_k \right)}{|X \cap Y|} \quad (1)$$

where 1_k is an indicator function taking the value of 1 if $Y_k \in X$ and 0 otherwise, and P_k is the precision at k:

$$P_k(X, Y) = \frac{|X \cap Y_{1:k}|}{k} \quad (2)$$

---

[2]In literature on bilingualism, cognates are commonly defined as translations that have similar forms.

where $Y_{1:k}$ is the subset consisting of the first k responses in Y.

While average precision is frequently used in information retrieval, a shortcoming of this measure is that the order of responses in X does not matter. In practice, however, some of the responses can be several times more frequent than others. To account for this fact, we use a second measure, total variation distance v, which considers two probability distributions X' and Y', associated with the likelihoods of responses in X and Y, respectively: e.g., $X' \sim \{\mathcal{L}(X_i), 1 \le i \le |X|\}$, where the likelihood is proportional to the response frequency in the human data (and later, to the association score in our model). The measure v is then defined as:

$$v_n(X, Y) = \frac{1}{2} \sum_{r_i \in \{X \cup Y_{1:n}\}} \left| X'(r_i) - Y'_{1:n}(r_i) \right| \tag{3}$$

Sometimes response r_i does not appear in one of the lists; if, e.g., r_i is not in Y, we take $Y'(r_i) = 0$.

For both measures, we test two values of n: $n = 3$ to compare only the top three responses per cue in the data, and $n = |X|$ to compare the maximum possible number of responses per cue. Note that in the latter case, n varies per cue word, depending on the number of responses in X. We denote the respective measures as ρ_3, v_3, and ρ_{max}, v_{max}.

To focus on systematic differences between word associations and eliminate the noise from occasional responses and various word forms, in all the reported analysis we remove hapax legomena (responses that are only given by one participant) and lemmatize all the responses, using Frog (van den Bosch et al., 2007) for Dutch and NLTK WordNet lemmatizer (Bird et al., 2009) for English.

3.2 Same vs. different bilinguals

First, we test if our measures are sensitive enough to find expected differences between sets of free association responses. For this, we compare the difference in responses from two different sets of bilinguals to the difference in responses from a single set of bilinguals at two different times – i.e., we expect more variation in the two response sets in the former case than in the latter, in line with vHdG's results. We use their data, in which one group of bilinguals, B_1, performed the free association task twice ($B_{1\text{-}1}$ and $B_{1\text{-}2}$), while another group performed it only once (B_2). We

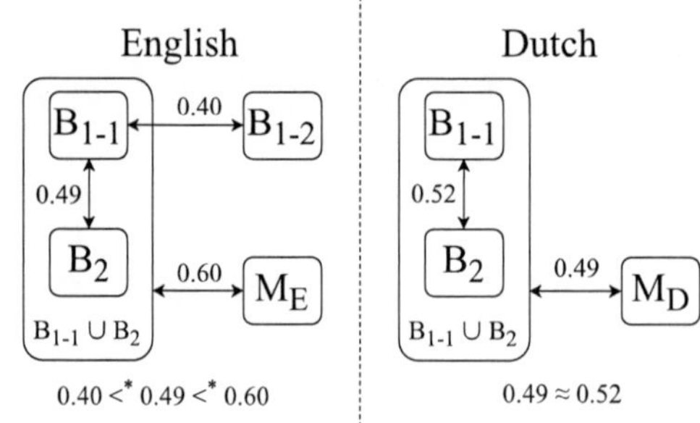

Figure 1: Distances (in terms of v_3) between the responses given by different groups of participants.

then expect that $\rho_3(B_{1\text{-}1}, B_{1\text{-}2}) < \rho_3(B_{1\text{-}1}, B_2)$,[3] and the same for v_3, ρ_{max}, and v_{max}. We compute the ρ and v values for responses given by vHdG's bilinguals to each of the 58 cue words.[4] Figure 1 (left panel) shows the distances in terms of v_3 only (the differences in distances on the three other measures are *more* pronounced). We statistically compare the distances using Wilcoxon signed-rank test on pairwise differences per cue word. The results confirm our prediction on all measures: mean $\rho_3(B_{1\text{-}1}, B_{1\text{-}2}) = 0.35$ is less than mean $\rho_3(B_{1\text{-}1}, B_2) = 0.47$ ($p = .002$); for v_3, the respective means are 0.40 and 0.49 ($p = .003$); for ρ_{max}, the means are 0.38 and 0.49 ($p = .004$); for v_{max}, they are 0.35 and 0.46 ($p = .002$). The consistency of the observed differences across the four measures suggests that the same set of bilinguals gives more consistent responses across sessions than two different sets of bilinguals, and this effect cannot be explained by random variation. Ideally, we would carry out a similar analysis for monolingual speakers, but individual-level data for monolingual speakers is not available at the moment.

3.3 Bilinguals vs. English monolinguals

Given that our measures are sensitive to differences across response populations, we can now turn to our main goal of verifying differences in the responses of non-native speakers (that is, Dutch–English bilinguals tested in English) compared to native English speakers. We expect more consistency in the responses given by the two groups of bilinguals ($B_{1\text{-}1}$ vs. B_2), compared to bilinguals vs.

---

[3]Responses in the second session ($B_{1\text{-}2}$) may be biased, so we use $B_{1\text{-}1}$ in comparisons to B_2 here and to other sets below.

[4]For consistency, two cues that did not appear in English association norms were excluded from all analyses.

monolinguals ($B_{1\text{-}1} \cup B_2$ vs. M_E);[5] see Figure 1 (left panel). (For English monolingual responses M_E, we use the University of South Florida association norms: Nelson et al., 2004.) The results confirm our prediction: mean $\rho_3(B_{1\text{-}1}, B_2) = 0.47$ is less than mean $\rho_3(B_{1\text{-}1} \cup B_2, M_E) = 0.63$ ($p = .003$); for v_3, the respective means are 0.49 and 0.60 ($p = .014$); for ρ_{max}, the means are 0.49 and 0.65 ($p = .002$); for v_{max}, they are 0.46 and 0.60 ($p = .002$). In short, despite the high variation in bilinguals' responses, there is still significantly more consistency between groups of bilinguals than between monolinguals vs. bilinguals.

3.4 Bilinguals vs. Dutch monolinguals

Finally, we check whether the difference reported in the previous section is only observed in bilinguals' L2 (English), or is also found in their L1 (Dutch). Intuitively, we expect little difference between the responses of Dutch monolinguals and Dutch–English bilinguals tested in Dutch. In other words, there should be a similar degree of consistency in the responses given by, on the one hand, the two groups of bilinguals ($B_{1\text{-}1}$ vs. B_2), and on the other hand, by bilinguals vs. monolinguals ($B_{1\text{-}1} \cup B_2$ and M_D); see Figure 1 (right panel). (For Dutch monolingual responses M_D, we use the Dutch association norms from De Deyne et al., 2013, while the Dutch bilingual data is available from vHdG's experiment.) Statistical tests again confirm our predictions: mean $\rho_3(B_{1\text{-}1}, B_2) = 0.47$ is not different from mean $\rho_3(B_{1\text{-}1} \cup B_2, M) = 0.51$ ($p = .601$); for v_3, the respective means are 0.52 and 0.49 ($p = .148$); for ρ_{max}, they are 0.50 and 0.56 ($p = .243$); for v_{max}, they are 0.47 and 0.51 ($p = .625$).

To summarize our human data analyses, we have shown quantitatively that Dutch–English bilinguals give systematically different responses in English (their L2) from English monolinguals. While such a difference has long been observed, to our knowledge we are the first to statistically analyze this difference and show that it is greater than the inconsistency in responses across participants. Besides, this difference is specific to bilinguals' L2, as we did not observe it in bilinguals' L1 Dutch.

4 Computational model

We develop a computational model intended to investigate the difference found above between bilinguals and monolinguals in free association. Our hypothesis is that bilingual associations in L2 are influenced by their L1 through connections between the lexicons of their two languages. We create a bilingual Dutch–English semantic network as a weighted directed graph G with a set of nodes N, where N consists of cue and response words obtained from (monolingual) word association norms in the two languages: De Deyne et al. (2013) for Dutch and Nelson et al. (2004) for English.[6] We next describe the various types of edges connecting the nodes, and the spreading activation mechanism used as a retrieval mechanism.

4.1 Edge types and weights

Dutch and English associative edges, which connect nodes within the same language, effectively create two monolingual sub-networks.

L1 associative edges (DA) start at a Dutch cue word and end at all its Dutch responses, based on the monolingual Dutch association norms. The edge weights are proportional to conditional probabilities $p(response|cue)$ obtained from the norms.

L2 associative edges (EA) are created the same way, using the English association norms. The two resulting sub-networks are then connected to each other with two following types of edges.

Translation equivalent edges (TE) connect nodes that are translations of each other. Translations are obtained from two dictionaries: FreeDict[7] and dict.cc.[8] In many cases a node n has more than one translation (e.g., a and b). To determine which one is more frequent, we use OpenSubtitles,[9] a bilingual corpus of Dutch–English subtitles (Lison and Tiedemann, 2016). Word alignment was performed on a random sample of 50 million sentences using the method of Liang et al. (2006), and conditional probabilities of each Dutch–English and English–Dutch translation were extracted. If a and b are translations of node n, edges E_{na} and E_{nb} are weighted proportionally to the conditional probabilities $p(a|n)$ and $p(b|n)$.

Cognate edges (CG) are placed between translation equivalents that have similar orthographic

---

[5] We use $B_{1\text{-}1} \cup B_2$, as this combined data set provides more responses for the comparison; using $B_{1\text{-}1}$ or B_2 instead gives very similar results.

[6] All words were lemmatized, and hapax legomena and multiword responses were removed.

[7] http://freedict.org

[8] http://www.dict.cc

[9] http://www.opensubtitles.org

forms. Cognates are believed to enjoy a special status in bilinguals (van Hell and de Groot, 1998; Voga and Grainger, 2007). These edges are defined using a similarity measure S, which is complementary to the normalized Levenshtein distance (Ciobanu and Dinu, 2013). Given two words w_i and w_j, S is computed as:

$$S(w_i, w_j) = 1 - \frac{L(w_i, w_j)}{\max(|w_i|, |w_j|)} \quad (4)$$

where $L(w_i, w_j)$ is the Levenshtein distance between the words, and $|w|$ is the number of characters in w. We consider w_i and w_j to be cognates when they are translation equivalents in our dictionary, and $S(w_1, w_2) \geq 0.5$. This rather low threshold was chosen to capture cognates that are spelled differently due to morphological or etymological reasons, yet are similar in their pronunciation: *swell–zwellen*, *photography–fotografie*, etc.

Finally, we consider two extra types of edges, which connect English nodes to each other. As we mentioned earlier, there is some evidence that bilinguals tend to produce more orthographic and syntagmatic responses in their non-native language, and the following types of edges are intended to test whether this is a systematic effect.

Orthographic edges (OR) connect English words with similar spelling; they are weighted using the measure S defined above. We chose a higher threshold than for cognates, 0.75, to prevent the English network from becoming too dense. Here, for simplicity we assume that word spelling captures not only orthographic, but also phonological similarity between words, although in principle, phonological edges could be added as an independent type in the model.

Syntagmatic edges (SY) reflect collocations or pairs of words that frequently co-occur. Sometimes participants produce syntagmatic responses in the free association task, such as *duty–free*, *opportunity–take*, or *apple–red*. While our DA and EA edges capture such responses, there is some evidence that bilinguals produce more of these in their non-native language, so we add these SY edges. Specifically, we consider the most frequent bigrams and trigrams (one million each; from the Corpus of Contemporary American English: Davies, 2008), convert trigrams into skip-bigrams (*take _ opportunity*), and exclude stopwords (using the NLTK list: Bird et al., 2009) and words that do not appear in the English free association norms. For each

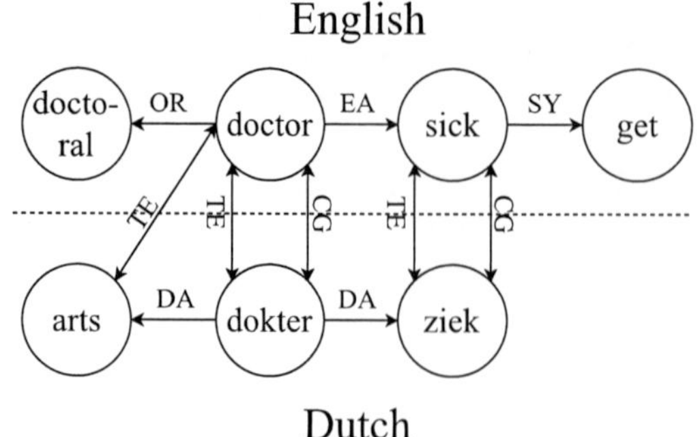

Figure 2: A part of the bilingual network.

pair of words, we compute their total number of co-occurrences in both bigrams and skip-bigrams, $F(w_1, w_2)$, and their total individual frequency, $F(w_1)$ and $F(w_2)$. Each weight for SY edge E_{ij} is set proportional to the respective conditional probability:

$$p(w_j|w_i) = \frac{F(w_i, w_j)}{F(w_i)} \quad (5)$$

Figure 2 shows a small part of the bilingual network with various types of edges.

4.2 Normalization of edge weights

We further weight each *type* of edges differently, to reflect their relative importance in the spreading activation process. These relative weights are the main parameters of our model. The model has six edge weight coefficients κ: κ_{DA}, κ_{EA}, κ_{TE}, κ_{CG}, κ_{OR}, and κ_{SY}, set as discussed in Section 5.2.

We normalize the edge weights of all outgoing edges of each node n to sum to 1, so that n passes on to its neighbors collectively the same amount of activation that it received. To do so, we first consider all outgoing edges of n a particular type – e.g., DA. We normalize the weights of all DA edges so that they sum to 1, and then multiply each weight by the respective coefficient, κ_{DA}. The same is done for all edge types. After that, we normalize the weights of *all* outgoing edges of n to sum to 1.

4.3 Retrieval algorithm

Given graph G with nodes N and edges E, the activation algorithm starts at a cue node n_{cue}, and activation spreads over edges to neighboring nodes, proportionally to the edge weights. This process is bounded in time by a parameter T, which is the upper limit of number of edges the activation can pass through. At the end, the model returns a ranked set of nodes (responses) $M = \{n_1, n_2, .., n_k\}$ and

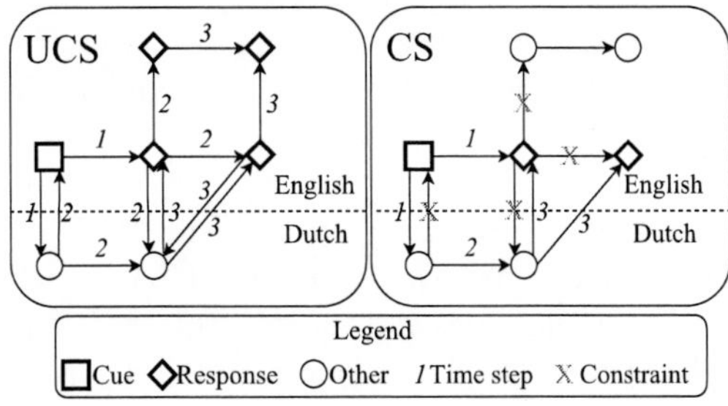

Figure 3: Spreading activation in the two models over a small part of bilingual network.

the respective likelihood value of each response, $\mathcal{L}(n_i)$:

$$\mathcal{L}(n_i) = \sum_{t=\{0..T\}} A^t(n_i) \qquad (6)$$

where $A^t(n_i)$ is the activation score of n_i at time t:

$$A^t(n_i) = \sum_{n_j \in \{N \setminus n_i\}} A^{t-1}(n_j) w(E_{ji}) \qquad (7)$$

where E_{ji} is the edge connecting n_j to n_i, and $w(E_{ji}) = 0$ if the two are not connected. Initially, $A^0(n_{cue}) = 1$; for all other nodes $A^0(n_i) = 0$.

5   Experimental setup

5.1   Task, models, and baselines

We test our model on the English free association task given to bilinguals in vHdG – i.e., Dutch–English speakers were given English cue words and asked to respond in English.

We consider two versions of spreading activation in the model, unconstrained and constrained (see Figure 3). In both versions, we set T – the maximum path length of spreading activation – to be 3, following the intuition that bilinguals may translate the English cue into Dutch (time $t = 1$), think of Dutch word associations ($t = 2$), and translate them back into English ($t = 3$).

In the **unconstrained version (UCS)** of the model, activation crosses *all* types of edges at each time step. Note that a T value of 3 enables activation to spread from the English to the Dutch subnetwork and back, but also allows activation to spread beyond the direct English associates. The next version of the model controls for this.

The **constrained version (CS)** simulates a bilingual who accesses direct English associates of the cue word, as well as English translations of direct Dutch associates of Dutch translations of the cue

word. That is, they combine their direct English associations with direct Dutch associations. At $t = 1$, activation passes from the cue node to its English associates and to its Dutch translations, via EA and TE/CG edges, respectively. At time $t = 2$, activation passes only from the just-activated Dutch nodes via DA edges to their Dutch associates. Finally, at $t = 3$, activation passes only from the newly activated Dutch nodes (the associates of cue translations) via TE and CG edges back to English nodes. Conceptually, this version implements a speaker who relies on the word translation mechanism.

Because we have shown that human bilingual responses to the English free association task differ from those of monolinguals, we need to compare our model's performance to a monolingual (English) baseline. The **association norms baseline (BASE-AN)** corresponds to the English word association data set itself: i.e., we use EA edges only in the English subnetwork and set the maximum path length $T = 1$. An improvement over BASE-AN ensures that our model is producing a better match to bilingual data than simply outputting English monolingual associations. We also use a second monolingual baseline with the same subnetwork and edges; this **spreading activation baseline (BASE-SA)** instead uses $T = 3$, as in our model. This setting enables access to indirect English associations of the cue word (as in our model), but only through English connections (unlike our model). Comparing our model to BASE-SA indicates any improvement we see in our model is due to accessing the Dutch subnetwork (our theoretical claim) and not simply due to making indirect associations in English.

5.2   Model evaluation

In the test task, the model receives a set of cue words and generates multiple responses to each cue. Only English nodes can serve as responses, and their probabilities are normalized to sum to 1. The model responses are compared to human data using the measures defined in Section 3.1.

Our main goal is to test which types of edges systematically contribute to predicting bilinguals' (non-native) free word associations, and which do not. We have six parameters of the model related to edge weights (κ weights for the six types of edges) and a relatively low number of test items (58 cue words). To prevent overfitting, we perform

Table 1: Distances between model and human responses (averaged per cue word and per iteration). Best performance for each measure is in bold.

	Avg. score			
	ρ_3	v_3	ρ_{max}	v_{max}
BASE-AN	0.63	0.60	0.65	0.59
BASE-SA	0.63	0.61	0.66	0.61
UCS	0.63	0.60	0.63	0.58
CS	**0.59**	**0.57**	**0.61**	**0.56**

cross-validation on our data set, initially fitting only some of the κ parameters. Specifically, we first determine the best weights for the word association edges (κ_{DA} and κ_{EA}, which are essential for the task) and for the cross-language edges (κ_{TE} and κ_{CG}, which ensure that activation can pass from English to Dutch and back). We later test whether adding other edge types (SY and OR) improves the model.

For cross-validation, we use the Monte-Carlo method with $10,000$ iterations: in each iteration, the 58 cue words are randomly split into 48 training items and 10 test items. For each training sub-sample, we consider values $\{0, 1, 5, 10, 20, 25\}$ for each edge weight ($\kappa_{DA}, \kappa_{EA}, \kappa_{TE}, \kappa_{CG}$), run a grid search to find the best combination, and choose the four combinations (one per evaluation measure) which minimize the distance between the human and the model responses. These combinations are then evaluated on the respective test sub-sample.

6   Results

6.1   Testing the basic model

Table 1 provides average cross-validation scores for the two baselines and the two models. Recall that our scores are *distances* from human data, so lower values are better. We see that BASE-AN is a stronger baseline than BASE-SA. The UCS model shows little to no improvement over the baselines, and we only consider the CS model henceforth. The CS model shows a noticeable improvement over the stronger BASE-AN baseline, of 0.03–0.04 in terms of absolute distances, an improvement of 5%–6%.

Although the best combinations of edge weights of the CS model differ per iteration, one of them appears much more frequently than the others, over $12,000$ times: $(\kappa_{DA}, \kappa_{EA}, \kappa_{TE}, \kappa_{CG}) = (10, 5, 20, 25)$. To determine whether this combination makes significantly better predictions than the baselines, we test it on the full data set with

responses to 58 cue words and run a series of Wilcoxon signed-rank tests (one per measure). The results show that the model (average scores $\rho_3 = 0.57$, $v_3 = 0.56$, $\rho_{max} = 0.60$, $v_{max} = 0.55$) is significantly better than both baselines on all measures, apart from v_3 when compared to BASE-AN.

The comparisons to the baselines show that the CS model, but not the UCS model, predicts bilingual responses better than simply using monolingual responses, and it does so by using edges that link translations across English and Dutch.

6.2   Testing the model with extra edges

Here we see if adding the further two types of edges – OR and SY – improves the model predictions. We use the CS model with the best parameter combination, $(\kappa_{DA}, \kappa_{EA}, \kappa_{TE}, \kappa_{CG}) = (10, 5, 20, 25)$. Again, we cross-validate the model, this time running a grid search to find the best weights of the extra edges only, κ_{OR} and κ_{SY}. We look for the most frequent parameter combinations. The combination of the best CS model without the extra edges – that is, $(\kappa_{OR}, \kappa_{SY}) = (0, 0)$ – is about as frequent as a particular combination with syntagmatic edges – $(\kappa_{OR}, \kappa_{SY}) = (0, 1)$, and both of these perform the same on the full data set. Thus, OR and SY do not improve the model's performance overall. We return to this issue in the discussion.

Note that both for the UCS and CS models, we start by first fitting the κ values for associative edges and cross-language (translation and cognate) edges, because the literature generally agrees that L2 speakers use the translation mechanism at least to some extent (e.g., Meara, 2009). The other two mechanisms – collocations and form similarity – are tested as *additions* to the model. Effectively, this makes our basic CS model implement the learner relying on word associations (DA and EA edges) and translation equivalence (TE and CG edges), but not on collocation patterns or orthographic similarity between L2 words. One could also design a model without cross-language edges – that is, relying on L2 word associations (EA edges) together with collocations and/or orthography (OR and/or SY edges), which we do not present in this study for the lack of space.

6.3   Best model and error analysis

Here we look in detail at the best CS model and provide an error analysis. (For simplicity, we consider the model without SY edges.) This model weights direct monolingual associations more in

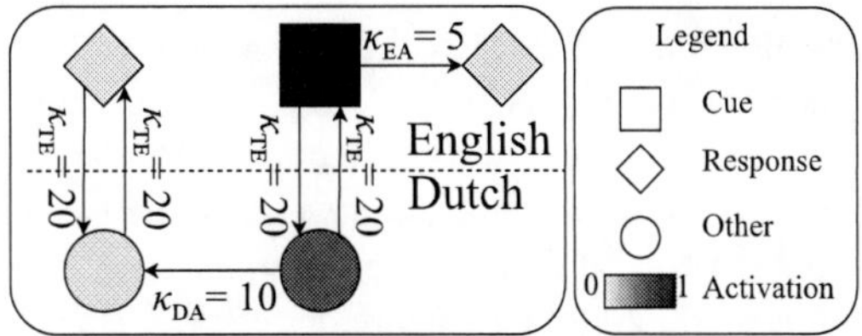

Figure 4: An illustration of the spreading activation in the best CS model (CG edges are not shown).

Dutch than in English: $\kappa_{DA} = 10$ vs. $\kappa_{EA} = 5$. Translation equivalents are also strongly connected to each other ($\kappa_{TE} = 20$), and cognates even more so ($\kappa_{CG} = 25$, which is *in addition* to the existing TE edge between them). This pattern of weights ensures that the translation operation is "cheap", and Dutch associates are readily activated; together these effectively make the contributions of English and Dutch associations similar in size. Figure 4 provides a toy example showing why this is the case. At the first step, a small share of the activation passes from the English cue to the English association, while the lion's share goes to the Dutch translation. At the second step, less than half of the activation at the Dutch translation proceeds to its associate; then in the third step, this activation is passed to the Dutch associate's translation.

This figure also shows why we cannot make conclusions about the contribution of a particular factor (e.g., translation equivalence, or the strength of English and Dutch word associations) based on the κ value of the corresponding edge type alone. Even though $\kappa_{TE} = 20$, $\kappa_{DA} = 10$, and $\kappa_{EA} = 5$, the contributions of native and non-native word associations to the final set of responses given by the model are similar, because English associations (the top right rhombus) are connected directly to the cue word, and the activation reaches them immediately upon the presentation of the cue, while Dutch associations (the top left rhombus) are further away from the cue word, and activation gets more dispersed as it passes through the network.

Table 2 shows the performance of the best model (vs. BASE-AN) for the best and worst cue words. For the majority of these cues the model is better than the baseline. For eight of these (*apple, block, bottle, chance, memory, season, shame, shoulder*), the improvement is consistent across the four measures. While the baseline relies on English word associations only, the model benefits from considering Dutch associations. This is because many

Table 2: Cue words for which the absolute difference between CS and BASE-AN is higher than 0.25 on at least one measure.

Cue	Improvement over BASE-AN			
	ρ_3	υ_3	ρ_{max}	υ_{max}
apple	0.56	0.41	0.30	0.32
block	0.11	0.21	0.33	0.24
bottle	0.56	0.40	0.23	0.15
chance	0.33	0.13	0.25	0.12
farm	0.00	0.06	0.60	0.27
flower	0.22	0.26	0.04	0.00
memory	0.17	0.34	0.03	0.16
season	0.83	0.55	0.63	0.52
shame	0.33	0.26	0.33	0.26
shoulder	0.67	0.34	0.29	0.20
attempt	−0.33	−0.03	−0.13	0.00
daughter	−0.33	−0.20	−0.33	−0.20
hospital	−0.33	−0.15	0.08	0.09
winter	0.00	−0.18	−0.25	−0.22

bilinguals' responses (e.g., *chance→possibility, shame→red, farm→farmer*) are missing in the monolingual data. In addition, some responses appear in the English monolingual data too, but are uncommon (e.g., *apple→pear, green*). In both cases, it is the translation edges that are responsible for the model's better performance.

Cue words on which the model is consistently worse than the baseline are *attempt, daughter*, and *winter*. For *hospital*, the model is only worse in predicting the top three responses. We find several reasons that may explain the model's errors.

Lack of data for some cues. The cue *attempt* is translated as *poging*, which activates a Dutch associate *probeersel* ['trial']. Because this word is not a cue in the Dutch association norms, all its activation is passed over its translation edges directly to *trial*, which yields relatively less activation for the more common response *suicide*.

Lack of word frequency information. For some cues (e.g., *hospital, winter*), the top human responses are words that are generally more frequent in English than are their Dutch translations (*nurse* vs. *verpleegster, spring* vs. *lente*).[10] In these cases, high frequency of English response words may lead speakers to rely more on English than on Dutch associations, which our model does not take

---

[10] As informed by relative word frequency information in English and Dutch subtitles (van Heuven et al., 2014; Brysbaert and New, 2009; Keuleers et al., 2010).

into account.

Language change. The data sets are not from the same time period (Dutch: 2010s; English: 1970s; bilingual: 1990s), so some responses that the model fails to reproduce may be attributed to language change: e.g., the response *duty→army* appears in the two older data sets, but not in the monolingual Dutch data, perhaps because conscription in the Netherlands was suspended in 1997.

7 Conclusion

We first showed that Dutch–English bilinguals in their L2 English give responses different from those of English monolinguals, but their L1 Dutch responses are not significantly different from those of Dutch monolinguals. While related observations have been reported in the literature (Wolter, 2001; Zareva, 2007; Antón-Méndez and Gollan, 2010; Hui, 2011, etc.), here we use a set of 58 cue words to demonstrate that this difference is consistent and is significantly larger than the difference between responses given by two groups of bilinguals.

Next, we presented a computational model based on a graph constructed from two monolingual word association data sets that were connected with additional cross-language edges. Our model predicts bilingual responses better than the monolingual baselines. The edge weights in the best model suggest that the contribution of L1 and L2 word associations is approximately equal in a group of Dutch–English bilinguals, and that translation equivalents (and cognates even more so) are strongly connected in the bilingual lexicon (in line with the findings on bilingual lexical access: e.g., Kroll et al., 2006; Dimitropoulou et al., 2011). Bilinguals may often translate L2 cues into L1, generate L1 associations, and translate them back into L1. In contrast, syntagmatic and orthographic responses that have been reported (e.g., Meara, 1978; Namei, 2004; Politzer, 1978) are not useful on the data set we used. Our results also suggest that it is not the case that bilinguals simply activate a broader cluster of L2 words and sample from those.

Van Hell and de Groot (1998) showed that bilinguals' responses might depend on the type of the cue word (e.g., noun–verb, abstract–concrete, cognate–non-cognate). As we intended to test how consistently various types of responses are produced across multiple cue words, we did not adjust the weights depending on the word type (except for cognates). Future research will consider enriching our network with such semantic and syntactic properties, as well as word frequency information. Another fruitful direction is to consider how to learn the association weights themselves, from textual and/or perceptual input (e.g., Griffiths et al., 2007; Gruenenfelder et al., 2015; Nematzadeh et al., 2016), rather than building them in from human norms; this would enable us to more realistically model the emergence of the bilingual lexicon.

Acknowledgments

We are grateful to Janet van Hell for sharing with us the word association data collected in her experiment with bilingual speakers.

References

Joshua T. Abbott, Joseph L. Austerweil, and Thomas L. Griffiths. 2015. Random walks on semantic networks can resemble optimal foraging. *Psychological Review* 122(3):558–569.

John R. Anderson. 1983. A spreading activation theory of memory. *Journal of Verbal Learning and Verbal Behavior* 22(3):261–295.

Inés Antón-Méndez and Tamar H. Gollan. 2010. Not just semantics: Strong frequency and weak cognate effects on semantic association in bilinguals. *Memory & Cognition* 38(6):723–739.

Nicole M. Beckage and Eliana Colunga. 2016. Language networks as models of cognition: Understanding cognition through language. In A. Mehler, A. Lücking, S. Banisch, P. Blanchard, and B. Job, editors, *Towards a theoretical framework for analyzing complex linguistic networks*, Springer, Berlin, Germany, pages 3–28.

Samuel Bilson, Hanako Yoshida, Crystal D. Tran, Elizabeth A. Woods, and Thomas T. Hills. 2015. Semantic facilitation in bilingual first language acquisition. *Cognition* 140:122–134.

Steven Bird, Ewan Klein, and Edward Loper. 2009. *Natural language processing with Python: Analyzing text with the natural language toolkit*. O'Reilly, Sebastopol, CA.

Alex Boulton. 2003. Transfer and translation in L2 word associations: Comparing learner data across languages. In J.-C. Bertin, editor, *24th GERAS conference: Transfert(s)*. GERAS. https://hal.archives-ouvertes.fr/hal-00114289.

Marc Brysbaert and Boris New. 2009. Moving beyond Kučera and Francis: A critical evaluation of current word frequency norms and the introduction of a new and improved word frequency measure for American English. *Behavior Research Methods* 41(4):977–990.

Alina M. Ciobanu and Liviu P. Dinu. 2013. A dictionary-based approach for evaluating orthographic methods in cognates identification. In R. Mitkov, editor, *Proceedings of the International Conference Recent Advances in Natural Language Processing (RANLP 2013)*. Association for Computational Linguistics, pages 141–147. http://www.aclweb.org/anthology/R13-1019.

Mark Davies. 2008. The corpus of Contemporary American English (COCA): 520 million words, 1990–present. https://corpus.byu.edu/coca/.

Simon De Deyne, Daniel J. Navarro, Amy Perfors, and Gert Storms. 2016. Structure at every scale: A semantic network account of the similarities between unrelated concepts. *Journal of Experimental Psychology: General* 145(9):1228–1254.

Simon De Deyne, Daniel J. Navarro, and Gert Storms. 2013. Better explanations of lexical and semantic cognition using networks derived from continued rather than single-word associations. *Behavior Research Methods* 45(2):480–498.

Robert M. DeKeyser. 2013. Age effects in second language learning: Stepping stones toward better understanding. *Language Learning* 63(s1):52–67.

Maria Dimitropoulou, Jon A. Duñabeitia, and Manuel Carreiras. 2011. Masked translation priming effects with low proficient bilinguals. *Memory & Cognition* 39(2):260–275.

Gemma B. Enguix, Reinhard Rapp, and Michael Zock. 2014. How well can a corpus-derived co-occurrence network simulate human associative behavior? In A. Lenci, M. Padró, T. Poibeau, and A. Villavicencio, editors, *Proceedings of the 5th workshop on Cognitive Aspects of Computational Language Learning (CogACLL 2014)*, Association for Computational Linguistics, pages 43–48. http://www.aclweb.org/anthology/W14-0509.

David Galea, Peter Bruza, Kirsty Kitto, Douglas Nelson, and Cathy McEvoy. 2011. Modelling the activation of words in human memory: The spreading activation, spooky-activation-at-a-distance and the entanglement models compared. In D. Song, M. Melucci, I. Frommholz, P. Zhang, L. Wang, and S. Arafat, editors, *Quantum Interaction: 5th International Symposium, QI 2011, Revised Selected Papers*, Springer, Berlin, Germany, pages 149–160.

Thomas L. Griffiths, Mark Steyvers, and Joshua B. Tenenbaum. 2007. Topics in semantic representation. *Psychological Review* 114(2):211–244.

Thomas M. Gruenenfelder, Gabriel Recchia, Tim Rubin, and Michael N. Jones. 2015. Graph-theoretic properties of networks based on word association norms: Implications for models of lexical semantic memory. *Cognitive Science* 40(6):1460–1495.

Li Hui. 2011. An investigation into the L2 mental lexicon of Chinese English learners by means of word association. *Chinese Journal of Applied Linguistics* 34(1):62–76.

Alice F. Jackson and Donald J. Bolger. 2014. Using a high-dimensional graph of semantic space to model relationships among words. *Frontiers in Psychology* 5. https://doi.org/10.3389/fpsyg.2014.00385.

Emmanuel Keuleers, Marc Brysbaert, and Boris New. 2010. SUBTLEX-NL: A new measure for Dutch word frequency based on film subtitles. *Behavior Research Methods* 42(3):643–650.

Judith F. Kroll, Susan C. Bobb, and Zofia Wodniecka. 2006. Language selectivity is the exception, not the rule: Arguments against a fixed locus of language selection in bilingual speech. *Bilingualism: Language and Cognition* 9(2):119–135.

Małgorzata Krzemińska-Adamek. 2014. Word association patterns in a second/foreign language – What do they tell us about the L2 mental lexicon? *Lublin Studies in Modern Languages and Literature* 38(1):141–153.

Percy Liang, Ben Taskar, and Dan Klein. 2006. Alignment by agreement. In R. C. Moore, J. Bilmes, J. Chu-Carroll, and M. Sanderson, editors, *Proceedings of the Human Language Technology Conference of the North American Chapter of the Association of Computational Linguistics*. Association for Computational Linguistics, pages 104–111. http://aclweb.org/anthology/N/N06/N06-1014.pdf.

Pierre Lison and Jörg Tiedemann. 2016. OpenSubtitles2016: Extracting large parallel corpora from movie and TV subtitles. In N. Calzolari, K. Choukri, T. Declerck, S. Goggi, M. Grobelnik, B. Maegaard, J. Mariani, H. Mazo, A. Moreno, J. Odijk, and S. Piperidis, editors, *Proceedings of Tenth International Conference on Language Resources and Evaluation*. European Language Resources Association. http://www.lrec-conf.org/proceedings/lrec2016/pdf/947_Paper.pdf.

Paul Meara. 1978. Learners' word associations in French. *Interlanguage Studies Bulletin* 3(2):192–211.

Paul Meara. 2009. *Connected words: Word associations and second language vocabulary acquisition.* John Benjamins Publishing Company, Amsterdam, the Netherlands.

Hyunjeong Nam. 2014. L1 mediation in L2 lexical access. *The Journal of Modern British & American Language & Literature* 32(3):39–65.

Shidrokh Namei. 2004. Bilingual lexical development: A Persian–Swedish word association study. *International Journal of Applied Linguistics* 14(3):363–388.

Douglas L. Nelson, Cathy L. McEvoy, and Thomas A. Schreiber. 2004. The University of South Florida free association, rhyme, and word fragment norms. *Behavior Research Methods, Instruments, & Computers* 36(3):402–407.

Aida Nematzadeh, Filip Miscevic, and Suzanne Stevenson. 2016. Simple search algorithms on semantic networks learned from language use. In A. Papafragou, D. Grodner, D. Mirman, and J. C. Trueswell, editors, *Proceedings of the 38th Annual Conference of the Cognitive Science Society*. Cognitive Science Society, Austin, TX, pages 1313–1318.

Robert L. Politzer. 1978. Paradigmatic and syntagmatic associations of first year French students. In V. Honsa and M. J. Hardman de Bautista, editors, *Papers in linguistics and child language: Ruth Hirsch Weir memorial volume*, Mouton, The Hague, the Netherlands, pages 203–210.

Klaus F. Riegel and Irina W. M. Zivian. 1972. A study of inter- and intralingual associations in English and German. *Language Learning* 22(1):51–63.

Ardi Roelofs. 1992. A spreading-activation theory of lemma retrieval in speaking. *Cognition* 42(1–3):107–142.

Massimo Stella, Nicole M. Beckage, and Markus Brede. 2017. Multiplex lexical networks reveal patterns in early word acquisition in children. *Scientific Reports* 7. https://doi.org/10.1038/srep46730.

Insup Taylor. 1976. Similarity between French and English words – a factor to be considered in bilingual language behavior? *Journal of Psycholinguistic Research* 5(1):85–94.

Antal van den Bosch, Bertjan Busser, Sander Canisius, and Walter Daelemans. 2007. An efficient memory-based morphosyntactic tagger and parser for Dutch. In Frank V. Eynde, Peter Dirix, Ineke Schuurman, and Vincent Vandeghinste, editors, *Selected papers of the 17th Computational Linguistics in the Netherlands Meeting*, LOT, Utrecht, the Netherlands, pages 99–114.

Janet G. van Hell and Annette M. B. de Groot. 1998. Conceptual representation in bilingual memory: Effects of concreteness and cognate status in word association. *Bilingualism: Language and Cognition* 1(3):193–211.

Walter J. B. van Heuven, Pawel Mandera, Emmanuel Keuleers, and Marc Brysbaert. 2014. SUBTLEX-UK: A new and improved word frequency database for British English. *The Quarterly Journal of Experimental Psychology* 67(6):1176–1190.

Madeleine Voga and Jonathan Grainger. 2007. Cognate status and cross-script translation priming. *Memory & Cognition* 35(5):938–952.

Brent Wolter. 2001. Comparing the L1 and L2 mental lexicon. *Studies in Second Language Acquisition* 23(1):41–69.

Alla Zareva. 2007. Structure of the second language mental lexicon: How does it compare to native speakers' lexical organization? *Second Language Research* 23(2):123–153.

Jeffrey C. Zemla and Joseph L. Austerweil. 2017. Modeling semantic fluency data as search on a semantic network. In G. Gunzelmann, A. Howes, T. Tenbrink, and E. Davelaar, editors, *Proceedings of the 39th Annual Meeting of the Cognitive Science Society*, Cognitive Science Society, Austin, TX, pages 3646–3651.

Experiential, Distributional and Dependency-based Word Embeddings have Complementary Roles in Decoding Brain Activity

Samira Abnar   **Rasyan Ahmed**   **Max Mijnheer**   **Willem Zuidema**

University of Amsterdam

{samiraabnar,rasyan21,max.mijnheer}@gmail.com, zuidema@uva.nl

Abstract

We evaluate 8 different word embedding models on their usefulness for predicting the neural activation patterns associated with concrete nouns. The models we consider include an experiential model, based on crowd-sourced association data, several popular neural and distributional models, and a model that reflects the syntactic context of words (based on dependency parses). Our goal is to assess the cognitive plausibility of these various embedding models, and understand how we can further improve our methods for interpreting brain imaging data.

We show that neural word embedding models exhibit superior performance on the tasks we consider, beating experiential word representation model. The syntactically informed model gives the overall best performance when predicting brain activation patterns from word embeddings; whereas the GloVe distributional method gives the overall best performance when predicting in the reverse direction (words vectors from brain images). Interestingly, however, the error patterns of these different models are markedly different. This may support the idea that the brain uses different systems for processing different kinds of words. Moreover, we suggest that taking the relative strengths of different embedding models into account will lead to better models of the brain activity associated with words.

1 Introduction

How are word meanings represented in the human brain? Is there a single amodal semantic system or are there multiple responsible for representing meanings of different classes of words? Recently, a series of studies have emerged showing that a combination of methods from machine learning, computational linguistics and cognitive neuroscience are useful for addressing such questions.

(Mitchell et al., 2008) pioneered the use of corpus-derived word representations to predict patterns of neural activation's when subjects are exposed to a stimulus word. Using their framework, a series of papers have evaluated various techniques of computing word representation models based on different assumptions, as we review in section 2.

Since these early successes, a range of new word embedding methods have been proposed and successfully used in a variety of NLP tasks, including methods based on deep learning with neural networks. (Baroni et al., 2014) and (Pereira et al., 2016) present systematic studies, showing that also behavioural data from psycholinguistics can be modelled effectively using neural word embedding models such as GloVe(Pennington et al., 2014) and word2vec(Mikolov et al., 2013). At the same time, studies in the area of vision have shown that deep learning models fit very well to the neocortical data (Cadieu et al., 2014; Khaligh-Razavi and Kriegeskorte, 2014) and they can help to better understand the sensory cortical system (Yamins and DiCarlo, 2016). To investigate how well the new word embedding models, and in particular the deep learning models, fare in helping to understand neural activation patterns in the domain of language, we now present a systematic evaluation of 8 word embedding models, listed in section 3, against the neuroimaging data from (Mitchell et al., 2008), following the experiments and primary results in (Mijnheer, 2017; Ahmed, 2017).

To address this goal, we take word embedding models designed based on different assumptions of how meanings of words can be represented and evaluate their performance on either the task of predicting brain data from word embeddings or the reverse, predicting word embeddings from brain data. The basic assumption here is that the better the performance of a model

Proceedings of the 8th Workshop on Cognitive Modeling and Computational Linguistics (CMCL 2018), pages 57–66,
Salt Lake City, Utah, USA, January 7, 2018. ©2018 Association for Computational Linguistics

is the more probable it is that the way the word embedding model is built reflects what happens in the human brain to understand a meaning of a word. In our experiments, we compare modern neural word embedding models with traditional approaches that are based on manually assigned linguistic word attributes, and neuro-inspired techniques based on sensory-motor features. Besides a large-scale evaluation of various word embedding models, we conduct a detailed error analysis to understand the differences between them.

The first research question we investigate is: *How well does each word embedding model allow us to predict neural activation patterns in human brain?* To answer this we measure how well different word embedding models can predict the brain imaging data. Taking this one step further, we also train our models in the reverse direction: to directly predict word embeddings from brain data.

The second research question that we investigate is: *What is the best word embedding model for predicting brain activation for different (classes of) nouns?* Maybe human brain uses different processes to understand meanings of different kind of words (Riddoch et al., 1988; Caramazza et al., 1990; Warrington and Shallice, 1984; Caramazza and Shelton, 1998). We do a qualitative analysis of our results to see whether different word embedding models are good in predicting the brain activation for different categories of nouns. The third question we address is *Which are the most predictable voxels in the brain for each word embedding model?* By answering this question we want to test the hypothesis that different areas of the brain are responsible for processing different aspect of the meaning of nouns. If different models have different performance either for different noun pairs or for different brain areas, the next step would be to find a way to integrate different models to build a model that better fits the brain data.

2   Related Work

The tradition of developing computational models to predict neural activation patterns given a representation of a stimulus such as a word was started by (Mitchell et al., 2008), who presented a model that quite successfully (with performance well above chance) predicted neural activation patterns associated with nouns, using a hand-designed set of 25 verbs (reflecting sensory-motor features) and computing representations for the nouns based on their co-occurrences with these verbs in a trillion-token corpus. Following this work, (Jelodar et al., 2010) proposed

using WordNet (Miller, 1995) instead of corpus statistics to compute the values for the 25 features introduced in (Mitchell et al., 2008), allowing them to deal with some of the ambiguity related issues. They find that a linear combination of their WordNet-based 25 features and the co-occurrence based 25 features of (Mitchell et al., 2008) improves the fMRI neural activity prediction accuracy. Devereux et al (Devereux et al., 2010) applied the framework to evaluate four different feature extraction methods, each based on a different source of information available in corpora. They show that general computational word representation models can be as good as sensory-motor based word representations. Later Murphy et al have done an extensive study comparing the performance of a different kind of corpus-based models on this task. In their experiments, a model that exploits dependency information outperforms the others (Murphy et al., 2012), in line with the results that we report below. (Binder et al., 2016) argue that it makes more sense to use experiment based word representations to model the mental lexicon. In (Fernandino et al., 2015) they use sensory-motor experience based attributes as elements of the word vectors to predict neural activation pattern for lexical concepts. The main difference of this approach with (Mitchell et al., 2008) is that rather than statistics from corpora they use actual human ratings to compute the feature values.

More recently, the success of neural network based approaches for learning word representations has raised the question whether these models might be able to partly simulate how our brain is processing language. Hence, it is now the time to revisit the challenge Tom Mitchell introduced and evaluate these new models with human brain neural activation patterns. In (Anderson et al., 2017) the performance of word2vec as the word representation model for predicting brain activation patterns is already evaluated. The goal of their experiment was to compare a text-based word representation with image-based models; our goal, instead, is to compare different neural word embedding models that are all text-based. Furthermore, (Xu et al., 2016) they compare the performance of various word embedding models, including neural based models and non-distributional models for both behavioural tasks and brain image datasets.

Taking the differences between all these different models for word representation into account, one can argue that they are not replaceable with each other. In (Dove, 2009) it is argued that both perceptual and non-perceptual features are important in decoding semantics. Moreover (Andrews et al., 2009) has suggested combining experiential and distributional models to learn word representations. In our experiments, we want to investigate whether the information encoded in different kind of word representations are mutually exclusive and hence, integrating them would result in a more powerful model.

There have also been some efforts to extend these models to analyze and understand brain activation patterns at sentence level (Wehbe et al., 2014) or at least in the context of a sentence rather than an isolated word (Anderson et al., 2016a). Moreover, some other related work abstracts away from the brain activation patterns and instead analyzes the correlation between the pairwise similarity of word representations in the brain and the computational model under evaluation (Anderson et al., 2016b).

In this paper, we stay with the original setup, using word representation models for predicting fMRI neural activation patterns, but go beyond existing work by presenting a systematic analysis and comparison of the performance of different kind of word representation models.

3 Experimental Setup

The main task in our experiments is to use a regression model to map word representations to brain activation patterns or vice versa. As the regression model, we employ a single layer neural network with $tanh$ activation. To avoid over-fitting we use drop-connect (Wan et al., 2013) with a keeping rate of 0.7 beside L2 regularization with $\lambda = 0.001$. In all the experiments we train the models for each subject separately. The training and evaluation are done with the leave-2-out method as suggested in (Mitchell et al., 2008). Where we train the model on all except 2 pairs and then evaluate the performance of the model on the left-out pairs. We do this for all possible combinations of pairs.

Neuroimaging Data Our experiments are conducted on the data from Mitchell et al. (2008) which is publicly available[1]. This is a collection of fMRI data that is gathered from 9 participants while exposed to distinctive stimuli. The stimuli consisted of 60 nouns and corresponding line drawings. Each stimulus was displayed six times for 3 seconds in random order, adding to a total of 360 fMRI images per participant.

Word Embedding Models In order to get insights about how human mental lexicon is built, we use a

wide variety of recently proposed word representation models. The word embedding models that we are exploring in our experiments are in two (non-exclusive) categories: experiential or distributional. In the experiential model, the meanings of the words are coded to reflect how the corresponding concept is experienced by humans through their senses. In the distributional models, the meaning of words is represented based on their co-occurrence with other words. These models can be either count-based or predictive (Baroni et al., 2014). The word representation models we will use are:

- **Experiential word representations**: Experiential word representations are suggested based on the fact that humans remember the meaning of things as they experience them. In (Binder et al., 2016) a set of 65 features are defined and crowdsourcing is used to rate the relatedness of each feature for each word. Thus, instead of computing the value of features using statistical data from textual corpora they use actual human ratings. We use the dataset introduce in (Binder et al., 2016). Since it contains only about 50% of the nouns in Tom Mitchell et al dataset, some of the experiments we report are with this limited noun set.

- **Distributional word embedding models**:

  - **Word2Vec**: Word2vec basically is a shallow, two layer, neural network that reconstructs the context of a given word. In our experiments, we use the skip gram word2vec model trained on Wikipedia (Mikolov et al., 2013).
  - **Fasttext**: Fasttext is a modification of word2vec that takes morphological information into account (Bojanowski et al., 2016).
  - **Dependency-based word2vec**: The dependency-based word2vec introduced in (Levy and Goldberg, 2014) is a word2vec model in which the context of the words is computed based on the dependency relations.
  - **GloVe**: GloVe is a count-based method. It does a dimensionality reduction on the co-occurrence matrix(Pennington et al., 2014).
  - **LexVec**: LexVec is also a count based method. It is a matrix factorization method that combines ideas from different models. It minimizes the reconstruction loss function that weights frequent co-occurrences heavily while taking into account negative co-occurrence (Salle et al., 2016b,a).

- **25 verb features**: Similar to experiential word

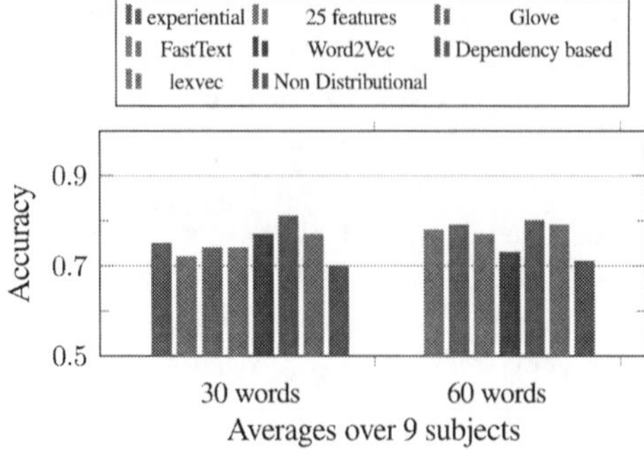

Figure 1: Results for the word to brain activation prediction task. (Chance is .5)

representations, this model is based on the idea that the neural representation of nouns is grounded in sensory-motor features. They have manually picked 25 verbs and suggested to use the co-occurrence counts of nouns with these 25 verbs to form the word representations (Mitchell et al., 2008).

- **non-distributional word vector representation**: (Faruqui and Dyer, 2015) have constructed a non-distributional word representation model employing linguistic resources such as WordNet(Miller, 1995), FrameNet(Baker et al., 1998) etc. In this model, words are presented as binary vectors where each element of the vector indicates whether the represented word has or does not have a specific feature. As a result, the vectors are highly sparse. The advantage of this model to distributional word representations is the interpretability of its dimensions.

4 How well does each word embedding model allow us to predict neural activation patterns in human brain?

To address the first research question, we train a separate regression model for each word representation model to compute the average brain activation corresponding to each word for a particular subject. Figure 1 illustrates the results of evaluating these models on the brain activation prediction task, using the leave-2-out methodology we discussed in section 3. For the sake of including the experiential word representations from (Binder et al., 2016) in our evaluations, we also conducted a set of experiments with only the nouns that were included in the experiential word representation collection. The good news is that all the models we are evaluating perform significantly above chance. The fact that the ranking of the models differs per

subject makes it difficult to make general conclusions about the best model. Overall, dependency-based word2vec, GloVe and 25 features model are the top-ranked models for at least one of the subjects.

Among neural word embedding models, dependency-based word2vec is achieving the best accuracy. This is in line with the results from (Murphy et al., 2012), where they showed that the corpus-based model considering the dependency relationships has the highest performance among corpus-based models. These authors report an accuracy of 83.1 (with 1000 dimensional word vectors). Somewhat higher still than the best dependency based word2vec, and the highest performance reported in the literature until now for a corpus-based model. The fact that fasttext and dependency based word2vec are performing better than word2vec might reflect the importance of morphological and dependency information. Comparing predictive models with count-based models, although count-based methods like GloVe and LexVec are beating simple word2vec, looking at the performances of fasttext and dependency based word2vec, we can conclude that the context prediction models can potentially perform better. Moreover, comparing the performance of the Experiential Model with 25 feature model, we see that the Experiential Model is doing slightly better on average while their ranking is different per subject. Either the higher number of features or the way feature values are computed could have led to the slight improvement in accuracy for the experiential model.

In both sets of experiments in Figure 1 the non-distributional word representation model has the lowest performance. The very high dimensionality of the brain imaging data versus the sparseness of non-distributional word vectors make training the regression model with these vectors much harder and this might be the primary reason for its low performance.

Next, instead of predicting brain activation patterns, we train the regression model to predict the word representation given a brain activation. Thus, we want to predict the stimulus word from the neural activation pattern in the brain. Evaluation is still based on the leave-2-out setup (so we still evaluate with 2 brain images and 2 word embeddings at each instance, making quantitative results comparable across experiments).

The results are shown in Figure 3. We expected the performance of the models on the reversed task, predicting word features from brain activation, to be somewhat similar to their performance on the main task, predicting brain activation patterns from word vectors. However, the results are surprising. For the

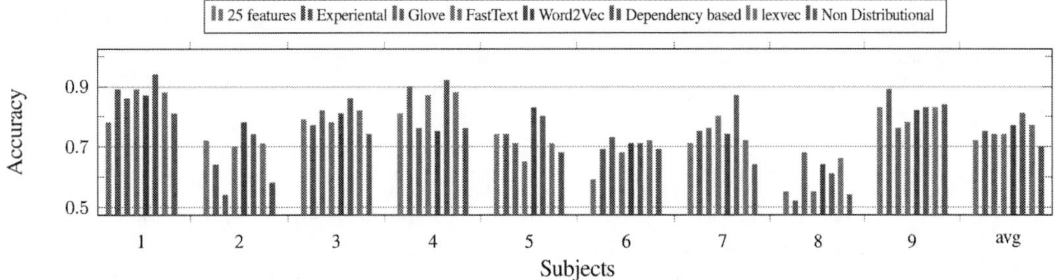

Figure 2: Results of different word representation models for the word to brain activation prediction task for the limited set of word, split per subject.

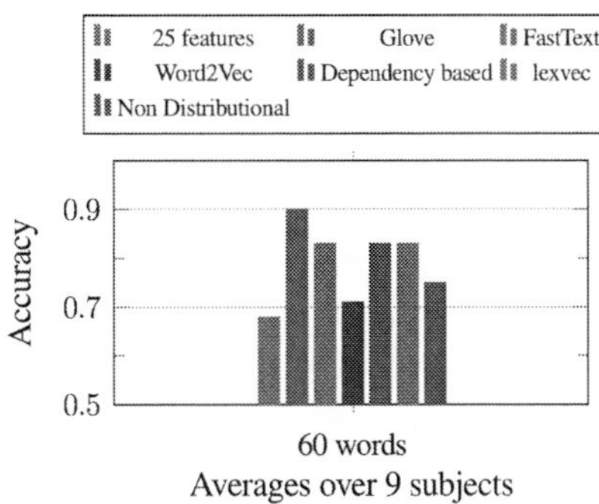

Figure 3: Results of different word representation models for the brain activation to word representation prediction task.

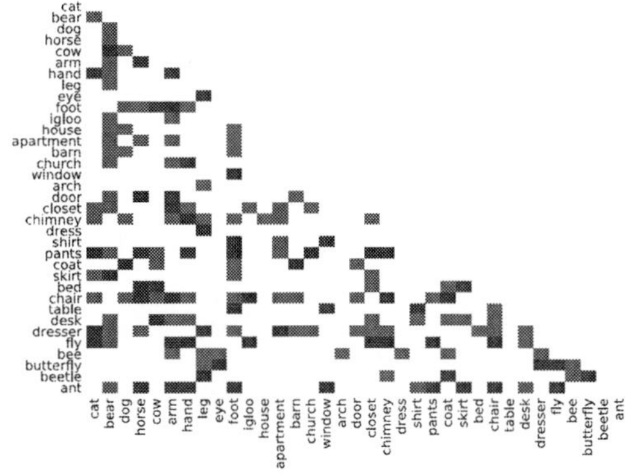

Figure 4: Mismatched word pairs for subject 1: 25 features model (red) vs experiential model (blue). In purple, word pairs confused by both models.

25 features model, the accuracy on the reversed task is much lower. This may be because of the way the feature vector for nouns is distributed in the space in this model. Or it could be that neural activation patterns do not encode all the necessary information to approximate these feature values. This could indicate that while the 25 features model is pretty useful in interpreting brain activation patterns it is not a plausible model to simulate how nouns are represented in the human brain. On the other hand, it seems that it is very easy to construct GloVe word vectors from brain activation patterns; this model achieves an accuracy of 90 percent. In (Sudre et al., 2012) accuracy of 91.19 percent is reported on the similar task on MEG data. GloVe is based on the distributional semantics hypothesis, and it is achieved by learning to predict the global co-occurrence statistics of words in a corpus. Hence, obtaining a high accuracy in the word prediction task using GloVe, supports the fact that the context of the words have a major role in the way we learn the meanings of the words. The important thing

to notice is that of course the more information we encode in the word representation the more powerful it becomes in predicting neural activation patterns as far as that information are relevant to some extent. However, this alone doesn't imply that the exact same information is encoded in the neural activation patterns. As we can see in our results, compared to GloVe, it's not that easy to reconstruct the Fasttext and dependency based word vectors from the brain activation patterns. What we can conclude, for now, is that while morphological and dependency information is helpful in learning word representations that are to some extent more similar to the neural representation of nouns in our brain. This information is not explicitly encoded in the brain activation patterns.

In the end, only comparing the accuracy of these models does not reveal much about the differences between them and does not mean that the model with the highest accuracy can replace all the others.

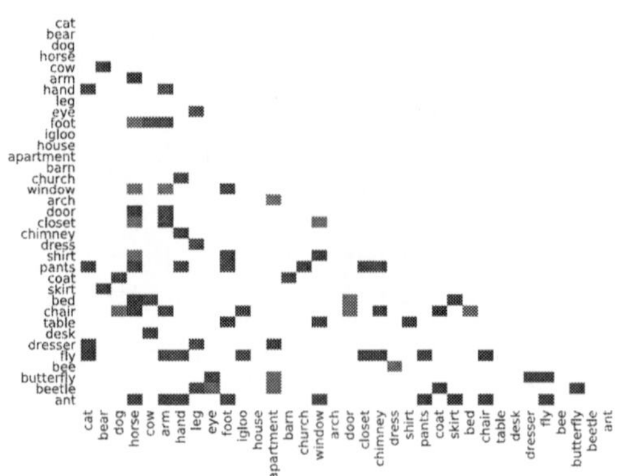

Figure 5: Mismatched pairs for subject 1: dependency based word2vec (red) vs experiential model (blue)

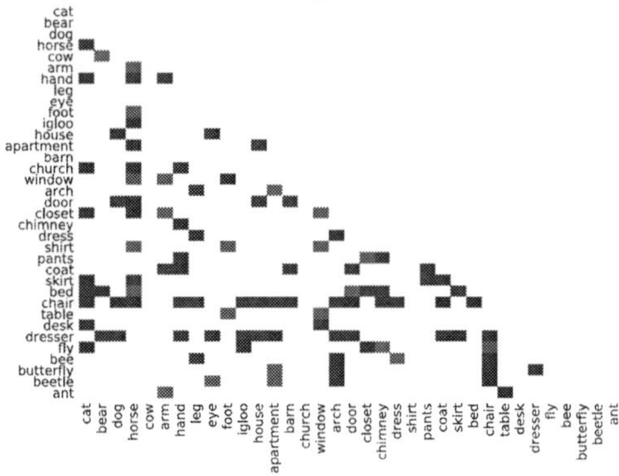

Figure 6: Mismatched pairs for subject 1: dependency based word2vec (red) vs word2vec (blue)

5 What is the best word embedding model for predicting brain activation for different (classes of) nouns?

In order to get more insights about the differences between the models, we look into the errors they make. It is informative to see whether each of these models is good at predicting neural activation pattern for a different group of noun pairs. We want to test the hypothesis of whether human brain uses different mechanisms for understanding meanings of different categories of words (Riddoch et al., 1988; Caramazza et al., 1990; Warrington and Shallice, 1984; Caramazza and Shelton, 1998). To investigate this we look into the miss matched noun pairs for each of the word representation models. We want to see which are the most confusing noun pairs for each model and measure the overlap between the errors the models make. This will reveal if these models are actually encoding different kinds of information.

Figures 4, 5 and 6 show the overlap between mismatched pairs for different models for subject

1. In these plots, the red color corresponds to the first model mentioned in the caption, the blue colour corresponds to the second model and the purple colour indicates the overlaps. While there is some overlap between the mistakes of the 25 features model and the experiential model, considerable number of mismatched pairs are not in common between them. One interesting fact about the 25 features model is that for some specific nouns ie. "bear", "foot", "chair", and "dresser", no matter what is its pair, discrimination performance is poor. eg. "bear" is not only confused with other animals, but also with some body parts, places and etc. We do not notice similar phenomena for the experiential model. This could be a side effect of using co-occurrence statistics from corpora to learn word representations and could show that for some reason the representations learned for these nouns are not distinguishable from other nouns. Looking into the noun pair mismatches of the experiential model and the dependency based word2vec in Figure 5, again we see a considerable amount of overlap. They both perform equally for discriminating among animals. But the experiential model makes more mistake about "body parts" and "insects". Comparing the dependency based word2vec with simple word2vec, in Figure 6 we observe similar patterns to Figure 4. As illustrated in the plot, discriminating some words eg. "chair" is difficult for word2vec while it's not the case for dependency based word2vec. It seems like both experiential attributes of nouns and the dependency information is helping in learning more distinguishable representations for nouns.

5.1 25 features vs experiential

As shown in Figure 1, the experiential model performs better than the 25 features model in average. Considering the fact that these two models are reflecting the same underlying theory, we might expect that if one of them is more accurate, it can replace the other. However, by looking into the difference between their mismatched pair, Figure 7, we observe that the mistakes these two models make are not completely overlapping: the nouns 'arm' and 'hand' are difficult to discriminate for both models, while 'chair' and 'house' are among the nouns with most mistakes for the 25 features model, and 'horse' and 'door' for the experiential model. For both models, most mismatches are in the category of body parts.

5.2 GloVe vs Dependency-based word2vec

We also compare the mismatch pairs for GloVe and dependency based word2vec as the two neural models

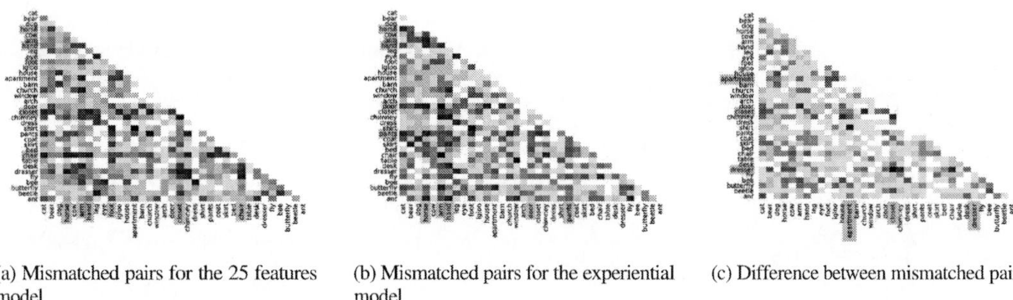

(a) Mismatched pairs for the 25 features model

(b) Mismatched pairs for the experiential model

(c) Difference between mismatched pairs

Figure 7: Comparing mismatched pairs for the 25 features model and the experiential model averaged over all subjects. Axes are the same as in figure 4.

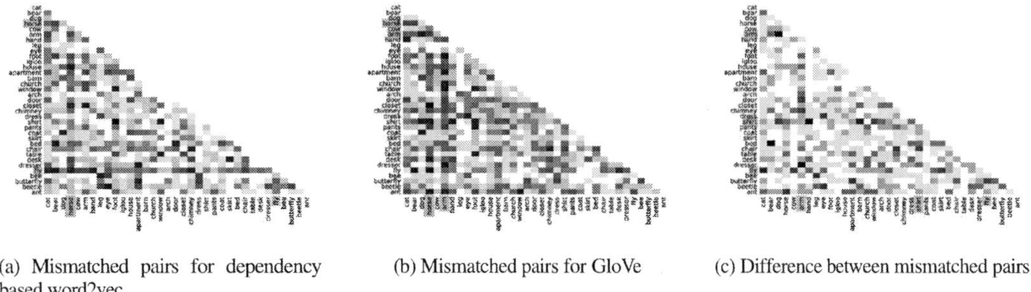

(a) Mismatched pairs for dependency based word2vec

(b) Mismatched pairs for GloVe

(c) Difference between mismatched pairs

Figure 8: Comparing mismatched pairs for dependency based word2vec and GloVe averaged over all subjects

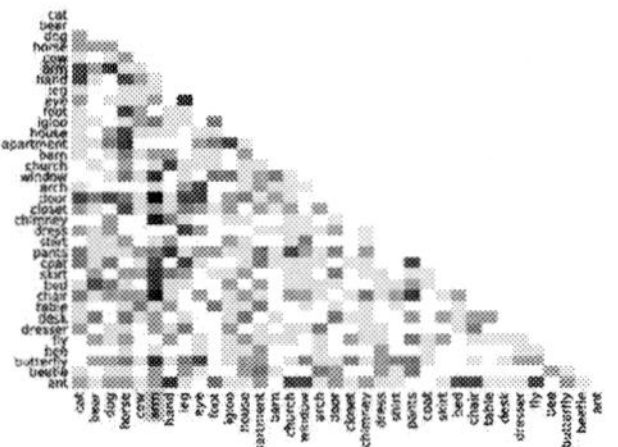

Figure 9: Difference of mismatched pairs for dependency based word2vec and experiential model

that achieve the highest accuracies in Figure 8. These two models are different both in the richness of the information they use to learn word representations, and also the way they use this information. In glove, the model is trained based on the global co-occurance of words whereas in word2vec word representations are learned based on the context of the words for each example locally. For GloVe, similar to the 25 features model and the experiential model, 'arm' is one of the hardest to discriminate nouns. But the 'body parts' category is not as confusing as for the experience based models. For the dependency-based word2vec, the patterns of errors are somehow different and the most difficult word seems to be 'fly'. This is because 'fly' can be either verb and noun, and since it is more frequent as a verb, the dependency-based

model is learning the representation of its verb form. For GloVe, this is not very problematic because it is only based on co-occurrence counts, thus an average representation is learned. In general, despite the fact that these two models are based on different assumptions their mismatches have more overlap than for the two experiential models. This may be a side effect of the fact that they both make fewer mistakes.

5.3 Experiential vs Dependency-based word2vec

The mismatched pairs of the experiential model and the dependency based word2vec and their difference is illustrated in Figure 9. The experiential model seems to have less prediction accuracy for noun pairs in the same category.

6 Which are the most predictable voxels in the brain for each word embedding model?

Each of the computational models of word representation we have employed to predict brain data is based on modelling different aspects of words meanings. Now we want to investigate if our brain is doing a combination of all these mechanisms and different groups of voxels in the brain are responsible for processing each aspect? One way to test this is to look into the predictability of different voxels with each

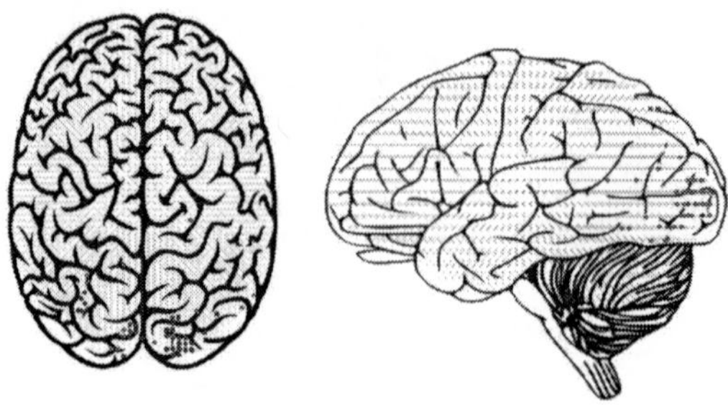

Figure 10: Most predictable voxels for dependecy based word2vec(red) and the experiential model(blue)

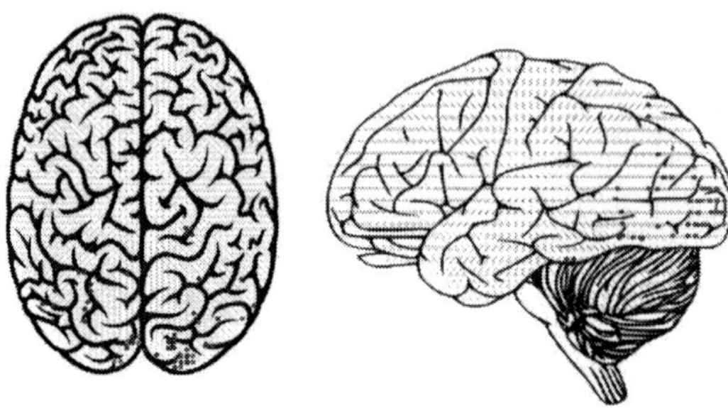

Figure 11: Most predictable voxels for dependecy word2vec(red) and word2vec(blue). Green dots are among the top 50 voxels of both models.

of these models. For this purpose, we have identified the top 50 most predictable voxels for each model. In Figure 10 you can see the 50 most predictable voxels for dependency-based word2vec and the experiential model. In Figure 11 you can see the 50 most predictable voxels for dependency-based word2vec and simple word2vec. The green colour indicates the common top voxels between the two models. From these figures, we can see that there is a lot more overlap between the dependency based word2vec and word2vec, compared to the experiential model.

A Mixed Model If each model is good at predicting the neural activation pattern for a different group of nouns/different groups of voxels, theoretically, it is possible to build a better model using an integrated model. In other words, we should be able to improve the accuracy of predicting neural activation patterns by employing a combined model. We conduct a new experiment by integrating the dependency based word2vec as a neural corpus-based word representation with the experience based models, ie the 25 verbs model and the experiential model. We expect the performance of the model to be a little bit higher than the dependency based word2vec. Our results indicate

that combining the dependency based word2vec with the experiential model linearly doesn't lead to an improvement in the accuracy over the limited set of words available in the experiential model. However, linearly combining the 25 feature model with the dependency based word2vec leads to an accuracy of 82 percent over the 60 nouns, which is 2 percent higher than the accuracy of the dependency-based model.

7   Discussion and Conclusion

Based on our systematic comparison, we can conclude that the deep learning models for learning word representations fit very well with brain imaging data. The existing models, like dependency based word2vec, are already beating the experiential word representation models that are particularly designed for the brain activation decoding tasks. Moreover, comparing the results of learning the mappings from words to brain activations and vice versa, convinces us that it is important to study the performance of the models in both directions to really understand what kind of information is encoded in the neural activation patterns for words.

Looking into the details of the performance of these models, it turned out that each of them makes different kinds of mistakes. One of the main problems of the corpus based distributional models that we have applied is that they do not account for different senses of the words. Hence, the representations they learn for words with more than one sense can be noisy and biased toward the most frequent sense. Taking the differences between the models into account, we build a model that combines the experience based word representation model with the dependency based word2vec. By linearly combining the 25 features model with the dependency-based model we are able to achieve a higher accuracy on the brain activation prediction task. We think it is possible to build new models upon the dependency based word2vec which also encode experiential information. One possible approach to achieve this goal is to train word embedding models in a multi-task learning framework with the downstream tasks that reflect different types of real-life experiences in addition to language modelling tasks.

In addition, in order to have a better understanding of the differences between different word representation models, we need to do a further analysis to answer the question *Which are the most predictable voxels in the brain for each word embedding model?*

8 Acknowledgement

The work presented here was funded by the Netherlands Organisation for Scientific Research (NWO), through a Gravitation Grant 024.001.006 to the Language in Interaction Consortium.

References

Rasyan Ahmed. 2017. How the brain gives meaning to words. Unpublished Bachelor thesis, Artificial Intelligence, University of Amsterdam.

Andrew J Anderson, Douwe Kiela, Stephen Clark, and Massimo Poesio. 2017. Visually grounded and textual semantic models differentially decode brain activity associated with concrete and abstract nouns. *Transactions of the Association for Computational Linguistics* 5:17–30.

Andrew James Anderson, Jeffrey R Binder, Leonardo Fernandino, Colin J Humphries, Lisa L Conant, Mario Aguilar, Xixi Wang, Donias Doko, and Rajeev DS Raizada. 2016a. Predicting neural activity patterns associated with sentences using a neurobiologically motivated model of semantic representation. *Cerebral Cortex* pages 1–17.

Andrew James Anderson, Benjamin D Zinszer, and Rajeev DS Raizada. 2016b. Representational similarity encoding for fMRI: Pattern-based synthesis to predict brain activity using stimulus-model-similarities. *NeuroImage* 128:44–53.

Mark Andrews, Gabriella Vigliocco, and David Vinson. 2009. Integrating experiential and distributional data to learn semantic representations. *Psychological review* 116(3):463.

Collin F Baker, Charles J Fillmore, and John B Lowe. 1998. The berkeley framenet project. In *Proceedings of the 36th Annual Meeting of the Association for Computational Linguistics and 17th International Conference on Computational Linguistics-Volume 1*. Association for Computational Linguistics, pages 86–90.

Marco Baroni, Georgiana Dinu, and Germán Kruszewski. 2014. Don't count, predict! a systematic comparison of context-counting vs. context-predicting semantic vectors. In *ACL (1)*. pages 238–247.

Jeffrey R Binder, Lisa L Conant, Colin J Humphries, Leonardo Fernandino, Stephen B Simons, Mario Aguilar, and Rutvik H Desai. 2016. Toward a brain-based componential semantic representation. *Cognitive neuropsychology* 33(3-4):130–174.

Piotr Bojanowski, Edouard Grave, Armand Joulin, and Tomas Mikolov. 2016. Enriching word vectors with subword information. *arXiv preprint arXiv:1607.04606* .

Charles F Cadieu, Ha Hong, Daniel LK Yamins, Nicolas Pinto, Diego Ardila, Ethan A Solomon, Najib J Majaj, and James J DiCarlo. 2014. Deep neural networks rival the representation of primate IT cortex for core visual object recognition. *PLoS computational biology* 10(12):e1003963.

Alfonso Caramazza, Argye E Hillis, Brenda C Rapp, and Cristina Romani. 1990. The multiple semantics hypothesis: Multiple confusions? *Cognitive neuropsychology* 7(3):161–189.

Alfonso Caramazza and Jennifer R Shelton. 1998. Domain-specific knowledge systems in the brain: The animate-inanimate distinction. *Journal of cognitive neuroscience* 10(1):1–34.

Barry Devereux, Colin Kelly, and Anna Korhonen. 2010. Using fMRI activation to conceptual stimuli to evaluate methods for extracting conceptual representations from corpora. In *Proceedings of the NAACL HLT 2010 First Workshop on Computational Neurolinguistics*. Association for Computational Linguistics, pages 70–78.

Guy Dove. 2009. Beyond perceptual symbols: A call for representational pluralism. *Cognition* 110(3):412–431.

Manaal Faruqui and Chris Dyer. 2015. Non-distributional word vector representations. In *Proceedings of ACL*.

Leonardo Fernandino, Colin J Humphries, Mark S Seidenberg, William L Gross, Lisa L Conant, and Jeffrey R Binder. 2015. Predicting brain activation patterns associated with individual lexical concepts based on five sensory-motor attributes. *Neuropsychologia* 76:17–26.

Ahmad Babaeian Jelodar, Mehrdad Alizadeh, and Shahram Khadivi. 2010. WordNet based features for predicting brain activity associated with meanings of nouns. In *Proceedings of the NAACL HLT 2010 First Workshop on Computational Neurolinguistics*. Association for Computational Linguistics, pages 18–26.

Seyed-Mahdi Khaligh-Razavi and Nikolaus Kriegeskorte. 2014. Deep supervised, but not unsupervised, models may explain it cortical representation. *PLoS computational biology* 10(11):e1003915.

Omer Levy and Yoav Goldberg. 2014. Dependency-based word embeddings. In *ACL (2)*. pages 302–308.

Max Mijnheer. 2017. Combining experiential and distributional semantic data to predict neural activity patterns. Unpublished Bachelor thesis, Artificial Intelligence, University of Amsterdam.

Tomas Mikolov, Kai Chen, Greg Corrado, and Jeffrey Dean. 2013. Efficient estimation of word representations in vector space. *CoRR* abs/1301.3781.

George A Miller. 1995. WordNet: a lexical database for english. *Communications of the ACM* 38(11):39–41.

Tom M Mitchell, Svetlana V Shinkareva, Andrew Carlson, Kai-Min Chang, Vicente L Malave, Robert A Mason, and Marcel Adam Just. 2008. Predicting human brain activity associated with the meanings of nouns. *science* 320(5880):1191–1195.

Brian Murphy, Partha Talukdar, and Tom Mitchell. 2012. Selecting corpus-semantic models for neurolinguistic decoding. In *Proceedings of the First Joint Conference on Lexical and Computational Semantics-Volume 1: Proceedings of the main conference and the shared task, and Volume 2: Proceedings of the Sixth International Workshop on Semantic Evaluation*. Association for Computational Linguistics, pages 114–123.

Jeffrey Pennington, Richard Socher, and Christopher D Manning. 2014. GloVe:global vectors for word representation. In *EMNLP*. volume 14, pages 1532–1543.

Francisco Pereira, Samuel Gershman, Samuel Ritter, and Matthew Botvinick. 2016. A comparative evaluation of off-the-shelf distributed semantic representations for modelling behavioural data. *Cognitive neuropsychology* 33(3-4):175–190.

M Jane Riddoch, Glyn W Humphreys, Max Coltheart, and Elaine Funnell. 1988. Semantic systems or system? neuropsychological evidence re-examined. *Cognitive Neuropsychology* 5(1):3–25.

Alexandre Salle, Marco Idiart, and Aline Villavicencio. 2016a. Enhancing the lexvec distributed word representation model using positional contexts and external memory. *arXiv preprint arXiv:1606.01283* .

Alexandre Salle, Marco Idiart, and Aline Villavicencio. 2016b. Matrix factorization using window sampling and negative sampling for improved word representations. *arXiv preprint arXiv:1606.00819* .

Gustavo Sudre, Dean Pomerleau, Mark Palatucci, Leila Wehbe, Alona Fyshe, Riitta Salmelin, and Tom Mitchell. 2012. Tracking neural coding of perceptual and semantic features of concrete nouns. *NeuroImage* 62(1):451–463.

Li Wan, Matthew Zeiler, Sixin Zhang, Yann L Cun, and Rob Fergus. 2013. Regularization of neural networks using dropconnect. In *Proceedings of the 30th international conference on machine learning (ICML-13)*. pages 1058–1066.

Elizabeth K Warrington and Tim Shallice. 1984. Category specific semantic impairments. *Brain* 107(3):829–853.

Leila Wehbe, Brian Murphy, Partha Talukdar, Alona Fyshe, Aaditya Ramdas, and Tom Mitchell. 2014. Simultaneously uncovering the patterns of brain regions involved in different story reading subprocesses. *PloS one* 9(11):e112575.

Haoyan Xu, Brian Murphy, and Alona Fyshe. 2016. Brainbench: A brain-image test suite for distributional semantic models. In *Proceedings of the 2016 Conference on Empirical Methods in Natural Language Processing*. pages 2017–2021.

Daniel LK Yamins and James J DiCarlo. 2016. Using goal-driven deep learning models to understand sensory cortex. *Nature neuroscience* 19(3):356.

Exactly two things to learn from modeling scope ambiguity resolution: Developmental continuity and numeral semantics

K.J. Savinelli
UCI Cognitive Sciences
`ksavinel@uci.edu`

Gregory Scontras
UCI Linguistics
`g.scontras@uci.edu`

Lisa Pearl
UCI Linguistics
& Cognitive Sciences
`lpearl@uci.edu`

Abstract

Behavioral data suggest that both children and adults struggle to access the `inverse` interpretation of scopally-ambiguous utterances in certain contexts. To determine whether the causes of both child and adult difficulty are similar, we extend an existing computational model of children's scope ambiguity resolution in context. We find that the same utterance-disambiguation mechanism is active in both children and adults, supporting the theory of developmental continuity. Moreover, because adult behavior requires an `exact` semantics for numerals, we also provide empirical support for this theory of linguistic representation.

Keywords: ambiguity resolution, developmental continuity, language acquisition, numerals, pragmatics, processing, Rational Speech Act model, scope, semantics

1 Introduction

Consider a scenario where two out of three horses jump over a fence. Is the utterance in (1) a reasonable description?

(1) *Every horse did<u>n't</u> jump over the fence.*

    a. $\forall \gg \neg$ (`surface` scope):
       None of the horses jumped over the fence.
    b. $\neg \gg \forall$ (`inverse` scope):
       Not all of the horses jumped the fence.

Adults typically endorse the *every-not* utterance as true, while children typically do not (Musolino, 1998; Lidz and Musolino, 2002; Musolino and Lidz, 2006; Musolino, 2006; Viau et al., 2010). This utterance is scopally ambiguous, involving multiple quantifiers (i.e., *every* and *n't*). Children's behavior is non-adult-like at five years old:

though the `inverse` interpretation in (1b) is true, five-year-olds still do not endorse the utterance.

Now, consider a scenario with only two horses, one of which successfully jumps. Is the *two-not* utterance in (2) a reasonable description?

(2) *<u>Two</u> horses did<u>n't</u> jump.*

    a. $\exists 2 \gg \neg$ (`surface` scope):
       There are two horses that didn't jump.
    b. $\neg \gg \exists 2$ (`inverse` scope):
       It's not the case that there are two horses that jumped.

Most adults would *not* endorse the utterance, despite the `inverse` interpretation in (2b) being true (Musolino and Lidz, 2003)—that is, it is not the case that two horses jumped (only one did).

This pair of findings underscores that not endorsing a scopally-ambiguous utterance when only the `inverse` interpretation is true occurs in both children and adults in different contexts. We might therefore wonder about continuity in the development of scope ambiguity resolution: is the cause of child utterance non-endorsement in an *every-not* scenario qualitatively similar to the cause of adult non-endorsement in the *two-not* scenario? If so, this similarity supports developmental continuity: children use the same mechanism as adults when understanding ambiguous utterances in context. The only difference would be that adults are better-equipped to deploy this mechanism, owing perhaps to increased domain-general knowledge and/or cognitive capacities, or to language-specific experience. In contrast, if the underlying causes are different for child and adult utterance non-endorsement, this would suggest developmental discontinuity: children are engaging in a fundamentally different process as they understand ambiguous utterances. So, the development of adult-like behavior would involve ac-

Proceedings of the 8th Workshop on Cognitive Modeling and Computational Linguistics (CMCL 2018), pages 67–75,
Salt Lake City, Utah, USA, January 7, 2018. ©2018 Association for Computational Linguistics

quiring a new mechanism for resolving ambiguity.

To choose between these accounts, we must understand utterance (non-)endorsement behavior. To that end, Savinelli et al. (2017) articulated a computational model of ambiguity resolution within the Rational Speech Act (**RSA**) framework (Goodman and Frank, 2016). The model demonstrated the central role of pragmatic factors over processing factors in explaining children's non-adult-like behavior in *every-not* contexts like (1). Here, we extend this same model to capture *two-not* utterance endorsement behavior in adults, identifying the factors that yield the experimentally-observed patterns of behavior.

We begin by reviewing the scope ambiguity resolution findings from Savinelli et al. (2017), together with the experimental results that informed the design of the computational model. Next, we consider the experimental findings from Musolino and Lidz (2003), where adults seem to behave like children in specific contexts. We then extend the model from Savinelli et al. (2017) to capture these new data, and demonstrate support for developmental continuity, with the same utterance-disambiguation mechanism active in both children and adults. Importantly, the complete range of experimentally-observed behavior can only be captured if adults represent *two* with an `exact` interpretation, an unexpected finding that informs the debate on numeral semantics.

2 Previous work: Modeling *every-not*

In the basic truth-value judgment task (**TVJT**) meant to assess children's scope disambiguation behavior, children first watch a scene acted out and hear a puppet produce a scopally-ambiguous utterance; then they are asked whether they would endorse the utterance as a true description of the scenario. Children typically do not endorse the ambiguous *every-not* utterance in the critical context where the `surface` interpretation is false but the `inverse` interpretation is true (e.g., a NOT-ALL scenario where two out of three horses jumped over a fence). This behavior has been interpreted as children failing to access the `inverse` scope interpretation that would make the utterance true.

Interestingly, various alterations to the task setup have yielded more adult-like behavior in children, with higher rates of endorsement for the *every-not* utterance. These experimental manipulations highlight at least three core factors (two

pragmatic, one processing) that underlie children's behavior in the TVJT: (i) *pragmatic*: expectations about the experimental world (e.g., how likely successful outcomes are), (ii) *pragmatic*: expectations about the Question Under Discussion (**QUD**; e.g., were `all` outcomes successful?), and (iii) *processing*: the accessibility of the `inverse` scope (i.e., the ease by which the logical form is either derived or accessed in real time).

To capture and independently manipulate the contributions of each of these factors, Savinelli et al. (2017) modeled ambiguity resolution for *every-not* utterances within the Bayesian RSA framework (Goodman and Frank, 2016). They found that when it comes to understanding non-adult-like behavior in the TVJT, there is likely a stronger role for the pragmatics of context management (as realized in prior beliefs about world state and QUD) than for grammatical processing (as realized in the prior on scope interpretations), although there may be a role for both. So, children's failure to endorse scopally-ambiguous *every-not* utterances in NOT-ALL contexts likely stems from their beliefs about the experimental world (e.g., whether actors are *a priori* likely to succeed) and about the topic of conversation (e.g., whether the conversational goal is to determine if `all` the actors succeeded), rather than an inability to grammatically derive or access the inverse scope interpretation in real time.

Perhaps most interesting was the prediction that the highest rates of utterance endorsement (i.e., adult-like behavior) occur when resolving the scope ambiguity is *irrelevant* for communicating successfully about the NOT-ALL world. This occurs when expectations about the world state favor total success, or when the QUD asks if `all`? of the actors succeeded. In either case, *both* scope interpretations serve to inform a listener, either that the *a priori* likely total-success world state does not hold or that the answer to the `all`? QUD is *no*.

The explanation for utterance non-endorsement (i.e., non-adult-like behavior) is similar: Savinelli et al. (2017)'s model predicts the lowest rates of utterance endorsement in NOT-ALL scenarios when neither interpretation is useful for successful communication, either because the interpretation is false (`surface`) or because beliefs about the pragmatic context render the interpretation uninformative (`inverse`). Thus, the TVJT utterance non-endorsement data previously used to demonstrate children's difficulty with `inverse` scope calculation in fact require no disambiguation at all if the goal is informative communication. Instead, children simply need the ability to manage the pragmatic context so they can recognize the potential informativity of these ambiguous utterances. Notably, considerations of pragmatic context have long played a role in the design and interpretation of the TVJT (e.g., Crain et al., 1996). Savinelli et al. (2017) take the extra step of formally articulating specific pragmatic factors and the role they play in children's apparent difficulty with ambiguous utterances in the TVJT.

3 Experimental *two-not* results

Musolino and Lidz (2003) (**ML2003**) demonstrated that adults are sensitive to some of the same experimentally-manipulated factors as children when it comes to endorsing scopally-ambiguous utterances. Like us, ML2003 were interested in developmental continuity: are child and adult ambiguity resolution behavior in context qualitatively similar? To investigate this, they conducted three TVJTs.

The goal of the first TVJT was to determine which interpretation adults preferred when they endorsed a scopally-ambiguous utterance in context. For example, adults heard *"Cookie Monster didn't eat two pizza slices"* in a context where both interpretations were true, such as Cookie Monster eating one of three available pizza slices (`surface`: *it's not the case he ate two* = true; `inverse`: *there are two he didn't eat* = true). Importantly, they were then asked to explain *why* they endorsed the utterance so that their preferred scope interpretation could be inferred. For example, if their answer referred to Cookie Monster eating only one slice, then it was assumed that they accessed the `surface` interpretation (`surface`: *he only ate one, so it's not the case he ate two*). However, if their answer referred to the two slices Cookie Monster did not eat, then it was assumed that they accessed the `inverse` interpretation (`inverse`: *there are two he didn't eat*). All participants endorsed the utterance, and their explanations indicated a strong surface scope bias (75% `surface`, 7.5% `inverse`, 17.5% unclear from explanation). ML2003 interpreted this finding as evdence that adults prefer the `surface` scope interpretation when both interpretations are true in context. It could then be that children's

non-endorsement behavior, if due to a preference for the `surface` scope interpretation, is driven by a stronger version of this same preference.

In the second TVJT, adults heard an utterance like (2) (e.g., *Two frogs didn't jump over the rock*) in two different contexts. The first context included two actors (e.g., frogs), with one actor successfully completing the action (e.g., $frog_1$ jumping over the rock while $frog_2$ does not). In this 1-OF-2 context, the `surface` interpretation is false (only $frog_2$ did not jump, so it is false that two frogs didn't jump), but the `inverse` interpretation is true (only $frog_1$ did jump, so it is indeed not the case that two frogs jumped). Yet, adults had low endorsement (endorsement rate: 27.5%).

In the second context, there were four actors. For example, four frogs attempted to jump over a rock; two jumped ($frog_1$, $frog_2$) and two did not ($frog_3$, $frog_4$). In this 2-OF-4 context, the `surface` interpretation of the scopally-ambiguous utterance is true because $frog_3$ and $frog_4$ did not jump. However, the `inverse` interpretation is false because $frog_1$ and $frog_2$ did indeed jump. Here, adults had an endorsement rate of 100%.

ML2003 interpreted this asymmetry of endorsement between the two contexts as a strong `surface` scope preference in adults. According to this explanation, non-endorsement occurs in the 1-OF-2 context because only the `inverse` scope is true; in contrast, endorsement occurs in the 2-OF-4 context because only the `surface` scope is true. That is, both these patterns would result because adults favor the `surface` interpretation. While we find this account compelling, we note that there are other differences between the two contexts that might lead to the observed asymmetry. For example, it could be that the seemingly benign change from two to four total actors affects the pragmatic context. Another variable is the potential ambiguity present in the numeral semantics, which only occurs in the 2-OF-4 context.[1] In either case, exploring the effects of these factors in a formal model of TVJT behavior can clarify the process underlying utterance disambiguation.

Returning to the question of continuity, while the observable behavior appears qualitatively the same in children and adults (i.e., a non-endorsement preference when only the `inverse` scope is true), it remains unclear whether the underlying cause of this behavior is the same. To

---

[1] A topic discussed in more detail in the following section.

evaluate this, ML2003 conducted a third TVJT with adults in 1-OF-2 contexts, involving an experimental manipulation from Lidz and Musolino (2002) that children are known to be sensitive to. This manipulation is implemented as an explicit linguistic contrast clause before the scopally-ambiguous utterance, such as the bolded material in (3).

(3) **Two frogs jumped over the fence but** two frogs didn't jump over the rock.

Adults responded the same way as the children from Lidz and Musolino (2002), shifting to strong endorsement in the 1-OF-2 context (endorsement rate: 92.5%; cf. 27.5% endorsement without the explicit contrast). Yet, as ML2003 note themselves, it is not obvious *why* the adult endorsement rate increases when the linguistic contrast is present. According to ML2003, the linguistic contrast creates the positive expectation necessary to make the negation in the later clause felicitous (Wason, 1965; Musolino and Lidz, 2003). However, it remains unclear *how* exactly the context creates the positive expectation. There are multiple ways this information could impact the context. For example, the positive expectation could arise because of a change *either* in the pragmatic factor of world knowledge or in the pragmatic factor of the QUD. Specifically, the affirmative statement could alter the listener's beliefs about how successful frogs are known to be in the experimental world. This affirmative statement also potentially changes the listener's expectations about the QUD: because both frogs were successful before, the topic of conversation might now be focused on whether both frogs were successful again. Both these effects could generate a context that makes the negated clause more informative.

Without knowing the factors responsible for endorsement behavior, it is difficult to determine whether the same factors are operating in both children and adults, and whether the underlying representation of *two* matters. Computational modeling can help determine why these two behavioral patterns occur: (i) adult sensitivity to the pragmatic contrast manipulation, and (ii) asymmetry in endorsement behavior between 1-OF-2 and 2-OF-4 contexts in the absence of that pragmatic contrast. In the next section, we extend Savinelli et al. (2017)'s model of utterance disambiguation to handle these empirical data.

4   Modeling *two-not*

Savinelli et al. (2017)'s model of ambiguity resolution is conceived within the Bayesian Rational Speech Act (RSA) framework (Goodman and Frank, 2016), which views language understanding as a social reasoning process. A *pragmatic listener* L_1 interprets an utterance by reasoning about a cooperative *speaker* S_1 who is trying to inform a *literal listener* L_0 about the world. The model is a "lifted-variable" extension in which the ambiguous utterance's literal semantics gets parameterized by interpretation-fixing variables (e.g., the relative scope of the quantificational elements; Bergen et al., 2012; Lassiter and Goodman, 2013; Scontras and Goodman, 2017). Hearing an ambiguous utterance, the pragmatic listener L_1 reasons jointly about the true state of the world (e.g., how many frogs successfully jumped), the scope interpretation speaker S_1 had in mind (i.e., `surface`, `inverse`), as well as the likely QUD that the utterance addresses (e.g., did `all` frogs succeed?). To generate testable predictions, participant TVJT behavior is modeled as a *pragmatic speaker* S_2's (relative) endorsement of an utterance about an observed situation (cf. Degen and Goodman, 2014; Tessler and Goodman, 2016). That is, this model predicts whether a speaker S_2 would endorse the scopally-ambiguous utterance as a description of the observed state. S_2 decides this by reasoning about whether a pragmatic listener L_1 (who is reasoning about a speaker S_1 reasoning about a literal listener L_0) would arrive at the correct world state after hearing the utterance.

We take world states $w \in W$ to consist of a collection of n individuals (e.g., frogs), each of which either succeeds or fails at the relevant task (e.g., jumping over a rock). The world success baserate b_{suc} determines the probability that an individual will succeed. We assume a simple truth-functional semantics where an utterance u denotes a mapping from world states to truth values ($Bool = \{\texttt{true}, \texttt{false}\}$). We parameterize this truth function so that it depends on the scope interpretation $i \in I = \{\texttt{inverse}, \texttt{surface}\}$, $[\![u]\!]^i$: $W \rightarrow Bool$. We consider two alternative utterances $u \in U$: the `null` utterance (i.e., saying nothing at all, and so choosing *not* to endorse the utterance) and the scopally-ambiguous utterance `amb` (e.g., *"Two frogs didn't jump over the rock"*).

To fix the utterance semantics, we must consider potential ambiguity introduced by the numeral in cases where the number of relevant individuals n exceeds the numeral's value. For example, consider the positive utterance *"Two frogs jumped over the rock."* If we assign an `exact` ($=$) semantics to *two*, the sentence will be true only when two frogs succeeded. If we assign an `at-least` ($\geq$) semantics, the sentence will be true when two or more frogs succeeded. In worlds with only two frogs, the $=$ vs. $\geq$ distinction makes no difference: the sentence will be true in the world where both frogs succeed, and false in all other worlds. However, in a world with four frogs, the numeral semantics will define different truth-functional mappings. With the $=$ semantics, the sentence is true in any world where two frogs—but not more—succeed. With the $\geq$ semantics, the sentence is true in a larger set of worlds, where two or more frogs succeed.

To evaluate the potential contribution of utterance semantics to the 1-OF-2 vs. 2-OF-4 asymmetry, we consider two different sets of utterance alternatives, one with `amb`$_=$ and another with `amb`$_\geq$. So, $U_= = \{$`null`, `amb`$_=\}$ and $U_\geq = \{$`null`, `amb`$_\geq\}$. The utterance semantics in (4) shows that scope parameterization i only impacts the truth conditions for `amb` utterances.[2]

(4) *Utterance semantics* $[\![u]\!]^i$:

    a. $[\![$`null`$]\!]^i =$ `true`
    b. $[\![$`amb`$_{=/\geq}]\!]^i =$ if $i =$ `inverse`
                           then $[\![$`inverse`$_{=/\geq}]\!]$
                           else $[\![$`surface`$_{=/\geq}]\!]$

    where:
    $[\![$`inverse`$_=]\!] =$
        $\lambda w.\ \neg\exists!x\colon |x| = 2 \wedge x \subseteq$ `success(w)`
    $[\![$`surface`$_=]\!] =$
        $\lambda w.\ \exists!x\colon |x| = 2 \wedge x \nsubseteq$ `success(w)`
    $[\![$`inverse`$_\geq]\!] =$
        $\lambda w.\ \neg\exists x\colon |x| = 2 \wedge x \subseteq$ `success(w)`
    $[\![$`surface`$_\geq]\!] =$
        $\lambda w.\ \exists x\colon |x| = 2 \wedge x \nsubseteq$ `success(w)`

We consider five potential QUDs $q \in Q$, three from the original Savinelli et al. (2017) model: (i) "What happened with the frogs?" (`what-happened?`), (ii) "Did all the frogs succeed?" (`all?`), and (iii) "Did none of the frogs succeed?" (`none?`). We also consider two additional QUDs specific to the *two-not* utterance: (iv) "Did exactly two frogs succeed?" (`two`$_=$`?`), and

(v) "Did at least two frogs succeed?" (`two`$_\geq$`?`). The QUDs serve as projections from the inferred world state to the relevant dimension of meaning, so that $q : W \to X$ (Kao et al., 2014a,b). In practice, the QUDs establish partitions on the possible world states, as shown in (5). For example, the `all?` QUD partitions the world space in two: the unique world in which all frogs succeeded (`true`) and all other possible worlds (`false`).

(5) *QUD semantics* $[\![q]\!]$:

    a. $[\![$`what-happened?`$]\!] = \lambda w.\ w$
    b. $[\![$`all?`$]\!] = \lambda w.\ $`success`$(w) = w$
    c. $[\![$`none?`$]\!] = \lambda w.\ $`success`$(w) = \emptyset$
    d. $[\![$`two`$_=$`?`$]\!] = \lambda w.\ |$`success`$(w)| = 2$
    e. $[\![$`two`$_\geq$`?`$]\!] = \lambda w.\ |$`success`$(w)| \geq 2$

Literal listener L_0 has prior uncertainty about the true state, $P(w)$. L_0 updates beliefs about w conditioned on the the literal semantics, and restricts prior beliefs to those worlds that $[\![u]\!]^i$ maps to `true`. The function $\delta_{[\![u]\!]^i(w)}$ maps the Boolean truth value to a probability, 1 or 0.

$$P_{L_0}(w|u,i) \propto \delta_{[\![u]\!]^i(w)} \cdot P(w)$$

To capture the notion that communication proceeds relative to a specific QUD q, L_0 must infer not only the true world state w, but also the value of the QUD applied to that world state, $[\![q]\!](w) = x$.

$$P_{L_0}(x|u,i,q) \propto \sum_w \delta_{x = [\![q]\!](w)} \cdot P_{L_0}(w|u,i)$$

Speaker S_1 chooses an utterance u in proportion to its utility in communicating about the true world state w with respect to the QUD q, $[\![q]\!](w) = x$. Thus, the speaker maximizes the probability that L_0 arrives at the intended x from u. This selection is implemented via a softmax function (*exp*) and free parameter α, which controls how rational the speaker is in utterance selection.

$$P_{S_1}(u|w,i,q) \propto exp(\alpha \cdot log(L_0(x|u,i,q)))$$

Utterance interpretation happens at the level of the pragmatic listener L_1, who interprets an utterance u to jointly infer the world state w, the interpretation i, and the QUD q. We model ambiguity resolution as pragmatic inference over an underspecified utterance semantics (i.e., the interpretation variable i). To do this, L_1 inverts S_1's model, and so the joint probability of w, i, and q is proportional to the likelihood of S_1 producing utterance u given world state w, interpretation i, and QUD q, as well as the priors on w, i, and q.

$$P_{L_1}(w,i,q|u) \propto P_{S_1}(u|w,i,q) \cdot P(w) \cdot P(i) \cdot P(q)$$

---

[2] The `success()` function in (4) returns the set of successful outcomes in a world w.

To model the utterance endorsement implicit in TVJT, we need an additional level of inference. Pragmatic speaker S_2 observes the true world state w and selects u by inverting the L_1 model, thus maximizing the probability that a pragmatic listener would arrive at w from u by summing over possible interpretations i and QUDs q for world w.

$$P_{S_2}(u|w) \propto exp(log \sum_{i,q} P_{L_1}(w,i,q|u))$$

To generate model predictions for adult sensitivity to the pragmatic contrast manipulation and the 1-OF-2 vs. 2-OF-4 asymmetry, we fix various model parameters. For 1-OF-2 data, we set the number of individuals n to 2; for 2-OF-4 data, we set n to 4. The S_1 speaker rationality parameter $\alpha > 0$ is set to 2.5 (i.e., the same value in the *every-not* simulations in Savinelli et al., 2017). The priors $P(w)$ and $P(q)$ correspond to expectations for the discourse context (i.e., likely world states or QUDs). In the default case, we set these priors to be uniform over their possible values, with the individual success baserate b_{suc} set to 0.5 and the relevant QUDs having equal probability. The interpretation prior $P(i)$ corresponds to how easy it is to access the inverse scope interpretation. In the default case, P(inverse) = P(surface) = 0.5. Importantly, to better understand utterance endorsement behavior with scopally-ambiguous utterances, we can independently manipulate the values of the priors on W, Q, and I, and observe their impact on utterance endorsement.

5   Results

Recall the empirical phenomena we are trying to capture: (i) the dramatic increase in endorsement rates in the 1-OF-2 context when an explicit contrast is present, and (ii) the stark asymmetry in utterance endorsement rates between 1-OF-2 and 2-OF-4 contexts in the absence of that explicit contrast. We report results for each in turn.

5.1   The explicit contrast effect for 1-OF-2

Following Savinelli et al. (2017), we attempt to capture the increase in ambiguous utterance endorsement rates by systematically manipulating the pragmatic and processing factors, as implemented in the relevant priors.

For the world state prior (Figure 1, *left*), we manipulate baserate b_{suc}, which determines an actor's chance of success. Holding the QUD and scope priors at their default values, we see a marked increase in endorsement of the ambiguous utterance in the 1-OF-2 context as prior beliefs about frog success increase. Utterance endorsement is at its lowest (33%) when prior knowledge suggests that frogs are particularly unlikely to succeed; endorsement is at its highest (86%) when frogs are very likely to succeed.

For the QUD prior (Figure 1, *center*), we selectively favor specific QUDs by assigning a 0.9 probability to the favored QUD and dividing the remaining probability equally among the others. Since the `two?` QUDs are equivalent to the `all?` QUD in the 1-OF-2 context, we omitted the `two?` QUDs in the 1-OF-2 context. Holding the other priors at their default values, endorsement rates increase from favoring the `none?` QUD (35%) to favoring the `what-happened?` QUD (46%) to favoring the `all?` QUD (64%).

For the scope prior (Figure 1, *right*), we manipulate the prior probability of the `inverse` interpretation while holding the other factors at their default values. We see an increase in utterance endorsement as the probability of `inverse` increases, from a low of 40% to a high of 57%.

Each manipulation qualitatively captures the response pattern from ML2003, and replicates the results of Savinelli et al. for *every-not*. However, as observed by Savinelli et al., the pragmatic factors controlling world and QUD beliefs have a much more pronounced effect than the processing factor controlling scope access; the model's world prior baserate manipulation comes closest to capturing the experimentally-observed effect of explicit contrast manipulation (i.e., 27.5% base endorsement vs. 92.5% endorsement with the explicit contrast). We can amplify the effect of the world baserate manipulation by allowing it to interact with the other factors.

As discussed in Section 3, the early success explicit contrast manipulation possibly affects two aspects of the disambiguation calculus: it could increase expectations for success and shift the topic of conversation to whether total success was achieved again. Figure 2 plots the interaction of the world and QUD priors, together with the effect of scope. The low-endorsement baseline (27.5%) most likely results from low expectations for success ($b_{suc} = 0.1$) and QUD uncertainty (QUD: `uniform`), together with a moderate to low probability of accessing the `inverse` scope ($P(inv) = 0.1$ or 0.5). From this baseline, we implement

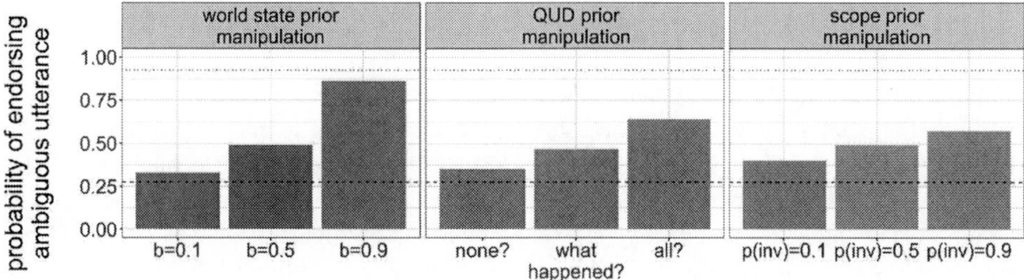

Figure 1: Model predictions for ambiguous *two-not* utterance endorsement (e.g., *Two frogs didn't jump over the rock*) in a 1-OF-2 context. Dotted lines represent experimentally-observed endorsement behavior in the absence (lower) and presence (upper) of an explicit contrast.

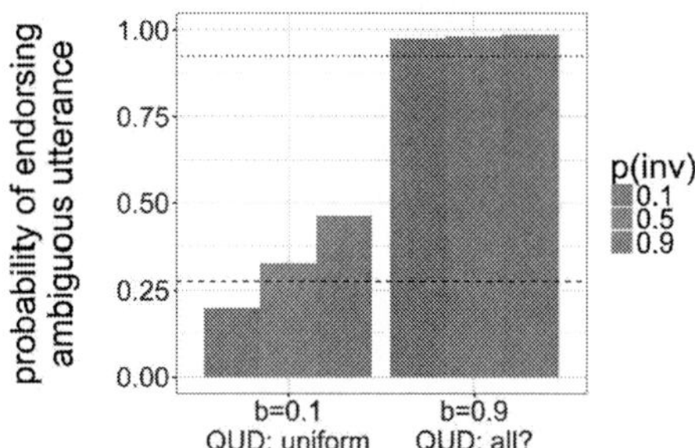

Figure 2: Model predictions for ambiguous *two-not* utterance endorsement in a 1-OF-2 context when multiple factors interact. Dotted lines represent experimentally-observed endorsement behavior in the absence (lower) and presence (upper) of an explicit contrast.

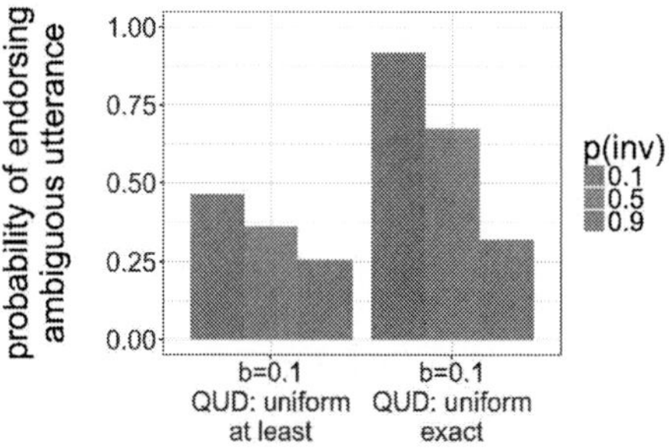

Figure 3: Model predictions for ambiguous *two-not* endorsement in a 2-OF-4 context.

the effect of the explicit contrast manipulation by increasing success expectations ($b_{suc} = 0.9$) and shifting the topic of conversation to whether total success occurred (QUD: all?). This manipulation results in a dramatic increase in utterance endorsement, irrespective of scope.

To summarize, if the explicit contrast clause impacts a listener's beliefs about the frogs' chance of success (increasing b_{suc}) or the QUD (favoring all?), then the model predicts the endorsement rate should increase. Notably, both of these manipulations make the *two-not* scopally-ambiguous utterance more informative for a listener. In the case of the the world state manipulation, *two-not*—under either scope interpretation—informs the listener that her prior beliefs about total frog success do not hold. Similarly with the QUD manipulation favoring all?, both scope interpretations answer this question in the negative (i.e., it is not the case that all (two) frogs succeeded).

5.2 The 1-OF-2 vs. 2-OF-4 asymmetry

If the factors identified for capturing the experimentally-observed effect of the ex-

plicit contrast are indeed active in utterance disambiguation (i.e., to validate their explanatory power), we would expect the very same factors and values to additionally capture the ceiling-level endorsement rate in the 2-OF-4 context without the explicit contrast.

Recall the baseline 1-OF-2 values from Figure 2: low expectations for success ($b_{suc} = 0.1$) and QUD uncertainty (QUD: uniform). To model the 2-OF-4 context, we change the number of actors n to 4 and additionally manipulate whether the exact ($=$) or at-least ($\geq$) semantics applies, as they diverge when there are more than two actors in the context (see section 4). This decision impacts both the utterance semantics and the relevant set of QUDs (e.g., if $\geq$ semantics gets used, then the two$_\geq$? QUD is included in the set of potential QUDs). As shown in Figure 3, we do indeed predict high endorsement with the same parameter value baseline, but only with exact utterance semantics and a low probability of accessing the inverse scope ($P(inv) = 0.1$). In this case, we find an endorsement rate of 92%.

6 Discussion

Our model of ambiguity resolution in context captures the effect of the explicit contrast manipulation observed in adults in ML2003, and notably also captured the same effect in children (Savinelli et al., 2017). This parallelism—sensitivity to the pragmatic context in both children and adults across different contexts—suggests that the same disambiguation mechanism is active in both children and adults. Adults seem better able to charitably interpret less supportive pragmatic contexts (i.e., the original *every-not* scenarios); yet, there remain scenarios (i.e., certain *two-not* contexts) where even adult abilities are exceeded. We interpret the common underlying mechanism as support for developmental continuity in scope ambiguity resolution, with no qualitative shift required.

In addition to supporting the developmental continuity hypothesis, this model also suggests *why* manipulations like the explicit contrast clause work. The pragmatic variables capture the explicit contrast manipulation because they create a situation where the ambiguous *two-not* utterance is still informative *despite* the ambiguity. When the utterance provides the listener with information that diverges from her prior beliefs, the ambiguous *two-not* utterance becomes more informative, more useful, and therefore more endorsable.

The model also seamlessly captures ML2003's results from the 2-OF-4 context: with the very same parameter values that yield low endorsement rates for 1-OF-2 contexts, the model predicts the high endorsement observed for 2-OF-4 contexts. The only change is increasing the number of relevant individuals from two to four. This exploration of the 1-OF-2 vs. 2-OF-4 contexts allows us to refine our understanding of the potential sources of child and adult behavior. Savinelli et al. (2017)'s findings suggested that pragmatic factors alone are capable of capturing the non-adult-like behavior in children and the extension in the current model captures the explicit contrast effect in adults; however, the processing factor of scope (in particular, disfavoring the inverse scope) is needed to account for ML2003's 2-OF-4 results. This finding supports ML2003's conclusion, namely that adults have a strong preference for surface interpretations of *two-not* utterances. Combined with the appropriate pragmatic context, that preference has the potential to drive the endorsement asymmetry between the 1-OF-2 and 2-OF-4 contexts. Whether this surface interpretation preference in *two-not* contexts is also something children share remains an open empirical question; experimental results for *every-not* do not answer this question definitively (Viau et al., 2010; Savinelli et al., 2017).

Importantly, the present model requires one more ingredient to account for the 1-OF-2 vs. 2-OF-4 difference in adult behavior: an exact numeral semantics (in contrast to an at-least semantics; cf. Geurts, 2006; Breheny, 2008; Spector, 2013; Kennedy, 2015). While the underlying utterance semantics is not something easy to manipulate in an experiment, it is exactly the kind of variable we can systematically explore in a computational model. By doing so here, we are able to show the necessity of an exact semantics in generating observable adult behavior. This provides empirical support, coming from computational modeling, for theories about the semantics of numerals. In particular, the only way to account for the observed adult behavior is if adults interpret *two* utterances as meaning exactly two.

To sum up, these findings underscore the complexity of information involved in interpreting scopally-ambiguous utterances, including the literal semantics of the utterances involved, processing factors that affect interpretation accessibility, pragmatic factors that affect the potential informativity of the utterance, and the recursive social reasoning between speakers and listeners. Here, we find evidence for the impact of both pragmatic and processing factors, and in particular how a specific confluence of values for these factors yields the observed adult utterance endorsement behavior in multiple contexts. The fact that pragmatic factors can have such a pronounced effect on their own accords with previous computational findings about the cause of children's utterance endorsement behavior in context, thereby highlighting the developmental continuity in pragmatic reasoning from childhood to adulthood. Moreover, the fact that the processing factor of scope access is crucial for explaining adult behavior in certain contexts motivates experimental work with children to see if their behavior is likewise affected by this processing factor in similar contexts. The fact that only the exact utterance semantics is capable of yielding the observed behavior provides empirical support in favor of this theory of representation for numerals. More broadly, we have demonstrated how computational modeling can help us refine our theories about different aspects of language, including theories of language understanding, language development, and language representation.

References

Leon Bergen, Noah Goodman, and Roger Levy. 2012. That's what she (could have) said: How alternative utterances affect language use. In *Proceedings of the Cognitive Science Society*. volume 34, pages 120–125. http://escholarship.org/uc/item/5f03m09d.

Richard Breheny. 2008. A new look at the semantics and pragmatics of numerically quantified noun phrases. *Journal of Semantics* 25(2):93–139. https://doi.org/10.1093/jos/ffm016.

Stephen Crain, Rosalind Thornton, Carole Boster, Laura Conway, Diane Lillo-Martin, and Elaine Woodams. 1996. Quantification without qualification. *Language Acquisition* 5(2):83–153. https://doi.org/10.1207/s15327817la0502_2.

Judith Degen and Noah D Goodman. 2014. Lost your marbles? the puzzle of dependent measures in experimental pragmatics. In *Proceedings of the Annual Meeting of the Cognitive Science Society*. volume 36, pages 397–402. http://escholarship.org/uc/item/97t2w1f3.

Bart Geurts. 2006. Take five: The meaning and use of a number word. In Svetlana Vogeleer and Liliane Tasmowski, editors, *Non-Definiteness and Plurality*, Benjamins, Amsterdam, pages 311–329. https://doi.org/10.1075/la.95.16geu.

Noah D Goodman and Michael C Frank. 2016. Pragmatic language interpretation as probabilistic inference. *Trends in Cognitive Sciences* 20(11):818–829. https://doi.org/10.1016/j.tics.2016.08.005.

Justine T Kao, Leon Bergen, and Noah D Goodman. 2014a. Formalizing the pragmatics of metaphor understanding. In *Proceedings of Annual Meeting of the Cognitive Science Society*. volume 36, pages 719–724. http://escholarship.org/uc/item/09h3p4cz.

Justine T Kao, Jean Y Wu, Leon Bergen, and Noah D Goodman. 2014b. Nonliteral understanding of number words. *Proceedings of the National Academy of Sciences* 111(33):12002–12007. https://doi.org/10.1073/pnas.1407479111.

Chris Kennedy. 2015. A "de-Fregean" semantics (and neo-Gricean pragmatics) for modified and unmodified numerals. *Semantics and Pragmatics* 8(1):1–44. https://doi.org/10.3765/sp.8.10.

Daniel Lassiter and Noah D. Goodman. 2013. Context, scale structure, and statistics in the interpretation of positive-form adjectives. In *Semantics and Linguistic Theory (SALT) 23*. pages 587–610. https://doi.org/10.3765/salt.v23i0.2658.

Jeffrey Lidz and Julien Musolino. 2002. Children's command of quantification. *Cognition* 84(2):113–154. https://doi.org/10.1016/S0010-0277(02)00013-6.

Julien Musolino. 1998. *Universal Grammar and the Acquisition of Semantic Knowledge: An Experimental Investigation into the Acquisition of Quantifier Negation Interaction in English*. Doctoral dissertation, University of Maryland, College Park. http://ling.umd.edu/assets/publications/Musolino_1998.pdf.

Julien Musolino. 2006. Structure and meaning in the acquisition of scope. In *Semantics in Acquisition*, Springer, pages 141–166. https://doi.org/10.1007/1-4020-4485-2_6.

Julien Musolino and Jeffrey Lidz. 2003. The scope of isomorphism: Turning adults into children. *Language Acquisition* 11(4):277–291. https://doi.org/10.1207/s15327817la1104_3.

Julien Musolino and Jeffrey Lidz. 2006. Why children aren't universally successful with quantification. *Linguistics* 44(4):817–852. https://doi.org/10.1515/LING.2006.026.

K.J. Savinelli, Gregory Scontras, and Lisa Pearl. 2017. Modeling scope ambiguity resolution as pragmatic inference: Formalizing differences in child and adult behavior. In *Proceedings of the Annual Meeting of the Cognitive Science Society*. volume 39, pages 3064–3069. https://mindmodeling.org/cogsci2017/papers/0579/paper0579.pdf.

Gregory Scontras and Noah D. Goodman. 2017. Resolving uncertainty in plural predication. *Cognition* 168:294–311. https://doi.org/10.1016/j.cognition.2017.07.002.

Benjamin Spector. 2013. Bare numerals and scalar implicatures. *Language and Linguistics Compass* 7(5):273–294. https://doi.org/10.1111/lnc3.12018.

Michael Henry Tessler and Noah D. Goodman. 2016. A pragmatic theory of generic language. http://arxiv.org/abs/1608.02926.

Joshua Viau, Jeffrey Lidz, and Julien Musolino. 2010. Priming of abstract logical representations in 4-year-olds. *Language Acquisition* 17(1-2):26–50. https://doi.org/10.1080/10489221003620946.

Peter C Wason. 1965. The contexts of plausible denial. *Journal of Verbal Learning and Verbal Behavior* 4(1):7–11. https://doi.org/10.1016/S0022-5371(65)80060-3.

Author Index

Abnar, Samira, 57
Ahmed, Rasyan, 57

Bicknell, Klinton, 10

Cho, Pyeong Whan, 19

Goldrick, Matthew, 19
Goodkind, Adam, 10
Gwilliams, Laura, 29

Jaffe, Evan, 1

Kalantari Dehaghi, Amir Ardalan, 46

Lewis, Richard L., 19
Linzen, Tal, 29

Marantz, Alec, 29
Matusevych, Yevgen, 46
Mijnheer, Max, 57
Miscevic, Filip, 35

Nematzadeh, Aida, 35

Pearl, Lisa, 67
Poeppel, David, 29

Savinelli, K.J., 67
Schuler, William, 1
Scontras, Greg, 67
Shain, Cory, 1
Smolensky, Paul, 19
Stevenson, Suzanne, 35, 46

Zuidema, Willem, 57